❋ WE HAVE THIS MINISTRY

The Kellogg Lectures
at The Episcopal Theological School
Cambridge, Massachusetts
February, 1958

WE HAVE THIS
MINISTRY

ROBERT N. RODENMAYER

HARPER & BROTHERS ❁ NEW YORK

❀ TO MY WIFE

✳ CONTENTS

❋ FOREWORD

Pastoral theology is one of the five major fields in the course of study of a modern theological seminary, the others being the Holy Scriptures, Church History, Theology and Ethics or Moral Theology. It used to consist, as some of us remember, of instruction in "sacred elocution" and construction of sermons, plus the reminiscences of a godly, successful, and senescent parish clergyman. Today, in most institutions, it is in a state of hopeful confusion. Dr. Richard Cabot and the Rev. Anton T. Boisen awakened all the churches to the need for special training in ministering to the sick and mentally disturbed, and it was discovered that clinical experience helped the young seminarian better to understand the average parishioner and himself. There has been a universal demand for education in parish administration, business methods, promotion and publicity, and the pastor's place in the community. Christian education, both of children and adults in the parish, has become so serious a concern in most churches as to require specialized training. As a result the pastoral field is in danger of breaking into a series of techniques unrelated to Theology and the Bible—a "practical" field, as though the Church's fundamental message and its living tradition were impractical!

This divorce of theory and life would be a most impractical and dangerous development. The Church's great periods of spiritual vitality have also been times of theological thinking. Wesley, St. Francis de Sales, St. Ignatius Loyola, Luther, Gregory, St. Augustine—all of them were theologians and

9

pastors. Pastoral theology is nothing other than the use of the Bible and Christian thought against the background of nineteen centuries of experience.

Professor Rodenmayer knows this. He always starts from what we know about God and His purposes for human beings. He takes into account the weaknesses of man and his glorious destiny which has been fulfilled in sainthood oftener than we think. He has disciplined himself to learn from psychologists, sociologists, and educators much of what is now known about people and their motives. As a working pastor, he has never hesitated to wear out shoe leather, automobiles, and his human frame to listen patiently to individuals in their happiness and their need.

Those who read his book will find that while it is divided into chapters on the Pastor, the Administrator, the Preacher, the Teacher, and the Priest, every chapter is about all these people for they are the same man. May the reader be helped through these pages to become a whole man, mature in Jesus Christ, ready for every good work.

SHERMAN E. JOHNSON

❀ WE HAVE THIS MINISTRY

ONE ❊ THE PASTOR

Pastor is an old word in our language carrying with it a recognized set of meanings and images. The figure of the Good Shepherd—the pastor image—immortalized in the Fourth Gospel, is strong in our cultural memory and often has given its name to parish churches. Many will remember Chaucer's lines in the prologue to "The Parson's Tale":

> Wide was his parish, houses far asunder,
> But he neglected not, for rain or thunder,
> In sickness or in mischief to visite
> The furthest in his parish, great and lyte,
> Upon his feet and in his hand a stave.
> This noble example to his sheep he gave,
> That first he wrought and afterwards he taught.
>
> . . .
>
> A better priest, I trow that nowhere none is;
> He sought after no pomp and reverence,
>
> . . .
>
> But Christe's lore, and his Apostles twelve,
> He taught, but first he followed it himselve.

But the lines fall on the ear with a certain nostalgia. This is not our world. Nor is the parson the modern man. The engineer, conqueror of space and matter, is the modern man. Aircraft companies and research foundations compete for his services. The new frontier is the sky. Even at ground level our world is changed and changing. It has shrunk to three or four large neighborhoods joined by the thoroughfares of the air. We no longer make pilgrimages to Canterbury on foot or muleback. And if we should go on pilgrimage we would wire ahead for reservations.

Parishes used to have boundaries. People lived and died in the same house. Now the parish boundary is an unknown and we have become a people on wheels. Our cars are more horse-powered, our trains more stream-lined, our airplanes more jet-propelled. We know our stuff and if our stuff proves inadequate we make better stuff. All of this would appear to be a rising curve from the time of the Renaissance, a short time ago historically, when inventions such as movable type, window glass, optical lenses, chimney flues, the mariner's compass, gunpowder and new weapons started us on a career to a brave new world. Much of this was good in effect and is still good. No one would wish to turn the clock backward but with all of the gains we seem to have created a new set of problems and a new setting for old ones.

Ours has been called the age of anxiety and while no age with its subtleties and its many levels of living can be caught in a word, this one carries a certain burden of truth. We have a higher proportion of recognized mental illness (partly because we know more about recognizing it), we have more people using sleeping pills and tranquilizers (because we invented them, of course, but the question why we needed to do so hangs in the air), we have more labor-saving devices in our homes but we sometimes have doubts about our use of the time saved. We have a new and useful science called psychiatry.

What I am saying is that the physical aspects of our world have changed considerably in a relatively short time, that we have discovered some new things about ourselves, that we ourselves are a little breathless and confused, but within all the changes and chances we are basically the same people with the same problems. Some years ago I moved from my first parish in a Massachusetts fishing town, a kitchen-door parish, to a larger one in an academic community. I did so with no little fear and inner trembling. What did I have to say to such people? I soon discovered that I had not really moved at all, only that the people had different names. Scratch a professor and you find a fisherman. He dresses differently, has more words to defend himself with, but he has the same problems, the same fears. He worries about the same things in the middle of the night.

The struggle of a little man to be decent most of the time, honest for the most part, liked and respected on the whole by those among whom he lives, to make a living, to meet his responsibilities and tragedies with some dignity and courage—this is the struggle of mankind. We may seem to live in "changing" times (when did they not?) or in any number of variously described states but the practical fact is that we live in *this* place in *this* time with *these* neighbors in *this* world. Let us begin here and look first at the pastor, his reason for being, and then a bit at his job of pastoring.

Why does a man go into the ministry? In common with physicians, lawyers, and plumbers, most of us might have done a number of other things for a living. A part of it, I suppose, is a desire to be used and, therefore, to have some meaning. It is a difficult thing to be really useful, to be geared into life. For the most part we experience this only at times. When I was a boy visiting on a farm we were awakened one night by shouts and the sound of running feet because a neighbor's barn was on fire. Everything was alarm and confusion. Pails were brought up, orders shouted, people formed themselves into a bucket brigade stretching from the local creek to the burning barn. I found myself, barefoot and excited, pressed into the line, passing a slopping bucket to the person ahead, turning back to grab the next one. Soon it settled into a rhythm, empty pails being rushed to the stream to start the chain again. From time to time a person would drop out of the line to rest a few minutes, his place taken by another, and then stand to again. After what seemed like a long time a part of the barn was saved and the sweaty, cinder-specked neighbors went home to catch a little sleep before the next day's work.

I was exhausted but in a sense fulfilled. I had been involved. I had known the feeling of direct, honest usefulness and it was good. Here is a clue, I think, a symbol both of the pull of the ministry and of its meaning. Dean Fosbroke, in my seminary days, once used the phrase "sober enthusiasm" to describe this feeling of honest usefulness in the Lord. It need not be so spectacular an occasion as a blazing hay barn; it might be something as quiet as patience or as silent and difficult as devotion.

But to be useful to what end? It seems to me that there are two poles to the ministry, God and the people of God. When one reads in applications to the seminary year after year the statements of men of various ages as to why they feel called to the ministry, one realizes afresh the difficulty of describing how this event takes place. Doubtless there are some of prophetic insight and moral conviction who, like Amos, seem to spring full-blown into the preaching ministry. Doubtless there are some who through some mystical experience feel compelled immediately to serve the Lord. Such experiences are not to be written off lightly though they may be difficult for others to understand, and no one knows how long a period of preparation may have preceded the decision. But for most of us it is a slow growth from speculation through trial into conviction. And even then there are doubts and there will be doubts.

Most of us come out of a Christian context—family, church involvement, reading, questioning—arrive at a point of decision and begin to prepare ourselves to go back into a Christian context in a somewhat different capacity. This is seldom, if ever, like walking upstairs in a serene progression. It is more often one step forward and two steps back; then, perhaps, three steps forward again into some small security. But one thing is always true: God speaks through the people of God. Always there is the support of the faithful community and often the person who sets the young man thinking and helps the older man change his mind does so unknown to himself. And this is sound theology. God the Holy Spirit is alive in His Church, leading, creating, and making new.

Behind every man of God there is a person or persons through whom God's leaven has worked. It may be the boy's own father; one of the lasting tributes to the ministry is the number of clergymen's sons who follow in their steps. It may be some other member of the family. It may be a lay person in the local church or it may be an encounter with a great person who saw the young man as he was and as he might be, and who took the time.

Most of us have our greats, a part of whose spirit we have borrowed. I can remember one of my early greats with vividness. That was Charles Henry Brent, my own bishop when I was a boy, and by then a world figure. I must have been about twelve when he came on a Sunday afternoon to the old Lyceum Theater in Rochester, New York, to talk about the League of Nations. I have no idea what possessed me to go by myself to listen to him on such a subject at such an age, but I did so.

I have no memory of the address but I have a clear memory of the man, strong, clear, forceful, somehow noble. Prompted by whatever it was, at the end of the speech I made my way through the orchestra pit to the stage, and found the speaker surrounded by a group of local dignitaries. With the brashness of twelve-year-olds I announced as if it were a matter of considerable importance that I would like to talk to him about going into the ministry. He received this intelligence gravely, indeed as if he thought it a matter of some importance, and said that he would like to hear me on the subject. Was I free at the moment? I was. Presently I found myself in the mayor's car with the Bishop, being driven to the home of his host and hostess. When we arrived there he asked if there were a room where he might talk with a young friend of his. We were ushered into the library where we spent an hour together on my problem. Again, I can remember none of the words but I can and do remember the man with clarity and gratitude.

Sometime later he received me as a postulant in a letter from shipboard when he was on his way to the first Conference on Faith and Order.

My course toward the ministry during the dozen years following that first encounter was the usual one. Many times I was beset by doubt and mistrust, several times I gave up the idea altogether, in college I seceded from religion root and branch for a while. But I never forgot that man or his effortless graciousness. He is one of the reasons—who can say how great?—that I am in this ministry.

I suppose that at the beginning of the course most of the men in our seminaries are not yet sure that this is for them. They come with hopes and fears and questionings, sometimes with a good measure of predogmatism, to find themselves in a rather strange new world—new studies, some of them alarming, new points of view, some of them not quite safe, new demands, new friends and associates, some of them appearing quite unlikely prospects for the Christian ministry. Sometimes the call, which at the time of leave-taking at home seemed genuine enough, shrinks almost to the vanishing point. The glory has departed, the vision has faded into common day.

Then it is that God speaks again through the ordinariness of the people of God. The community itself takes over, the same sort of Christian community out of which this man came. He begins to feel support and understanding, the health of new knowledge, the beginnings of usefulness, the yeastiness of the Spirit. And at the end of his seminary years the persons viewed with such alarm at the beginning have become, if not close friends, men known for their ways and respected for their abilities, men for whom there is a place in the ministry of the Church of God.

There are persons who come into the ministry after years of doing something quite different. A man may have thought seriously of this calling years ago and have given it up for a number of reasons. Then he marries, raises his children, and makes a living. But the old vision persists and he finds himself in seminary years later with the understanding and frequently with the financial support of his wife. Sometimes a mature man with a successful career comes into the ministry because of the insight and perception of his own pastor. It may be that the pastor's own ministry (unknown to either of them) has opened this door. I know of more than one man who in middle life has begun thinking toward the ministry because some tragic occurrence in his family was met with love and compassion by the local pastor.

Then there is the sort of person who sets out with a firm notion of what he is going to do in the world and who trips over the futility of his own success. I think of one young man now in the ministry, a bright and attractive person, who felt the influence of a good college pastor but nevertheless, after his college course, started up the ladder in a large industrial concern. He had been assigned to the refrigerator division, worked hard at it and earned promotion. After a year or so of this he turned up late one night on the doorstep of his college pastor where he was met with enthusiasm and welcomed in. He came, it turned out, to unburden his soul. After some general conversation he described his job and his prospects, both of them good, and came to the point in words something like this:

"You start in a large office and begin to learn the ropes. You learn who's who and what's what. You keep quiet and listen, you get your work in on time and after a while you begin to get noticed a little. You go from using a secretarial pool to sharing a secretary with three or four other rising young men. You move into a quieter office. . . . And I can see it all from here—the desk with the name plate on it, your own secretary, the new house in the suburb, the steady climb, the bright future." And finally at the end of the recital, "You know, the fact is I don't believe in refrigerators."

Much has been said and written recently about the changing concept of the ministry and of the minister's role. I have read these books and reports with interest and respect, and have taken part in some of the discussions. I have both a personal and professional concern for the young minister trying to find himself in a world he never made. I too feel this new demand, this accusation, this uncomfortableness. I think that we can expect some of the current inquiries to come up with sound and useful information, and for that we shall be grateful. But it seems to me that the new thing here is the method of testing rather than the data being tested. The problem is the old one—the tension between how a man sees himself and how others see him. *"Now there arose up a new king over Egypt, which knew not Joseph"* (Exod. 1:8).

The contemporary man of God has two opposite temptations. One is to prove that he is a modern man living in a real world. As such he must discover new techniques, read new books, learn a new language. He must specialize, buy new equipment, have a modern sort of office. He must impress the businessman that he is businesslike, that he knows what he is about. He must impress the world about him (and incidentally himself) that he is alive, aware, up-to-date, and not to be caught napping. This man has snap, he has verve, he has aggressiveness. In fact he is in danger of becoming a success.

The opposite temptation is the retreat into traditionalism, the gentle settling into "custom's oilèd groove," the make-believe that Chaucer's world is our world. This man says, in effect, "I am a member of a respected profession. My function is known, accepted, and appealed to. I am always welcome and needed, an eagerly-awaited father figure, a good shepherd, a comfort. Nothing really is changing or has changed." This man is Parmenides in a clerical collar. But nobody cares. He will not be challenged (in the root sense, please!); he will be more or less politely ignored.

Now there is some truth in both of these exaggerations. It is true that "new occasions teach new duties." It is true and necessary that the man of God deal relevantly with the world about him. It is true that new methods may be as practical in the ministry as in any other field. But it is untrue to confuse the method with the aim.

On the other hand, there is truth in the traditional approach. It is true that this person has a known place and represents a known function in our society, although in our novels and plays he appears more often as a moral censor or an upholder of things-as-they-are than as a good shepherd. He does stand on something. He does represent God, but God is always relevant.

There is another way of saying this. Consider the young man at the moment of ordination. He has read and discussed and listened and thought. He has written papers and passed examinations. He has dreamed and hoped and prayed. Now is the quietness of dedication, the inner resolve, the stirring of power. This is good and of God. Then, as in any commitment, the trouble begins. The world is not eager to hear his message, souls resist being saved, meetings are small. There seem to be a lot of routine, a lot of sameness, very few sparks among the stubble. Where has the dream fled? Let me read you a bit from the letter of a young man in the first year of his ministry. He wrote this letter to friends at the seminary.

"First, perhaps the biggest disappointment is this. You want to do so much more for your people than they will ask you to do —sick calls, prayers, teaching. You see yourself as a vehicle to display and explain God's love to men; they tend to see you as a moneymaker for the Church and a general handyman. I can see where it will be years before they (by instinct) call me when someone is sick or when a personal problem arises. I warn you, unless you find a completely different situation than I have, that your potential value to the souls in your care will not be utilized at the outset. Second, you will soon see the validity and necessity of the 'redemptive community' approach to a vital parish. But the average layman will think you are as screwy as a $4 bill. They have no idea what you mean."

Two real questions emerge: who *is* this man in the midst of all his roles—self-imposed and thrust upon him—and what is to nourish and sustain him in his lonely soul-searching, in the acid of self-distrust? When at the beginning of their senior year I ask students in the seminary to write an answer to the first question, Who is this man?, they come up with the same spectrum of replies that their elders report in response to questionnaires: the servant of God to do His will, the reconciler showing forth the healing love of God in Christ, the preacher of the good news of salvation, the witness-bearer in his own life, the teacher of the truth of God, the administrant of sacraments, a man concerned for the whole community—churched and unchurched. All of this is good, predictable, and encouraging. This is what the minister *is*, under God. But this is not necessarily what society —even a nominally Christian society—wants him to be. His people generally want him to be a great many other things: a crisp administrator, a competent youth leader but not neglectful of the older people, an organizer, a good mixer, a wise counselor, a strong preacher, a man of spiritual depth and intellectual power, an entertainer, an indefatigable caller, a model husband and father, a leading citizen.

Now it is only fair to say that there is some overlap in these two lists. One preaches the good news of salvation outside of the pulpit, one shows forth the healing love of God in Christ in some quite unlikely places. But there is a gap, certainly, between the two sets of roles for the minister. The solving of the problem, insofar as it is ever solved, is a process rather than an event. One has to experience, in little, a sort of "fall of man" before he can begin to make peace with reality. We have to lose some of our illusions about ourselves before we can see clearly. We must walk before we run, we must search before we can guide.

Before a man ever thinks of going into the ministry he has been blessed by God with certain gifts, attributes, and aptitudes. To these he adds his experiences—his personal history, good and bad—and his reflections on it. All of this, together with his hopes and plans and dreams, he offers when he is ordained, and again and again and again. All men will not be great preachers, perhaps not even good ones. All men will not have the kind of unperturbed openness and understanding that belongs to the good counselor. All men will not be able administrators. But each man, unless he tries too hard, will discover what he has been given and a little about how to give it back.

When Tom Sawyer and his friends Joe Harper and Huckleberry Finn decided to run away and be pirates on an island in the Mississippi they were abrogating, in a rather healthy and attractive way, the roles thrust upon them by society. After the adventure in piracy had thinned out a bit Tom stole home after dark to discover that he and his friends had been given up for dead. You will remember how the boys went to their own funeral and heard, to their astonishment, a sermon recounting their shining but previously unnoticed virtues. Can this be really I?

Each of us lives in a complexity of relationships. One can be at the same time father, son, husband, brother, neighbor, friend, citizen, and so on, and in each of these appear differently. Which is the real self? In a sense each of them and none of them. Each appearance conveys part of the whole person, while the man within the appearances, known only to God, is most truly the person he is in process of becoming. So with the man of God. He is a bundle of things, some of them in conflict with others, but he feels called to serve the Lord and His people in His Church. Slowly he prepares himself and is launched. In good time he will find his feet, he will discover something about what he can and cannot do, he will begin to grow up, he will make an offering.

One gets used to hearing about specialized ministries: the college ministry, the rural ministry, the urban ministry, the hospital ministry, the ministry to prisons. There are specialized things to be learned in any field, of course, but basically the ministry is what it is and a good man in one place will be adaptable and apt in another.

There is the other question: What supports this man, young or old, in his self-distrust? For it, too, is real. Elijah the man of God, fleeing from the wrath of Jezebel, says, *"It is enough; now, O Lord, take away my life; for I am not better than my fathers"* (I Kings 19:4). Even so. One knows the feeling of emptiness, of powerlessness. But God speaks quietly to Elijah in his bleakness and the prophet is restored. The text, I think, for the whole of one's ministry—good times and bad—is, *"Surely the Lord is in this place; and I knew it not"* (Gen. 28:16). Again and again we put our trust in the wrong things, the wrong people. We trust the world's ideals—money, power, success—forgetting that *"my grace is sufficient for thee; for my strength is made perfect in weakness"* (II Cor. 12:9). It is enough, but it is God's enough.

When I was a child I was taken to a hospital for an operation; nothing earth-shaking, tonsils as I remember, but I had to stay overnight and I was afraid. Further, my glasses had been commandeered so everything about me was in a blur. My pastor came to see me after visiting hours and I am sure he had never been more welcome to anybody. We talked a little, he said a prayer for me, and then, as he was leaving, added, "The hand that made you can hold you." It can and it does.

When we say that God speaks we mean that, as in the call to the ministry, God speaks through what He has given. I have no quarrel with those who say that God Himself speaks to them directly in words though I have had no such experience myself. I do know that there are times when old words said or read many times before suddenly take on a flash of meaning that changes everything. There was such an occasion in my early days as a pastor when I was called to minister to an old lady who was in great trouble. She was my spiritual superior and both of us knew it but quite simply and honestly she shared with her young pastor what her anxiety was. I did the best I could but it wasn't much; I hadn't lived long enough. Leaving her I went back to the parish church to say some prayers in my own need. While I was doing so the old familiar words from Deuteronomy popped into my mind—"underneath are the everlasting arms"—but with new meaning. I jumped to my feet and almost ran back to the home of the old lady and announced, "I have just discovered something!" "What is it?" she asked, smiling at my eagerness. "I have just discovered that the everlasting arms are underneath —not waving around in the sky—but underneath, where they have to be. You can't fall through into nothingness; that's where God is." She was not smiling now. Very quietly she said, "Thank you," and very quietly I left her. God had spoken to both of us.

Sometimes it happens without conversation and at the end of inner turmoil. I can remember with poignancy a time, again in my first parish, when I was beset with a feeling of my own unworthiness. The grounds for the feeling were ample enough, as always, but the cloud darkened the sky for days and darkened everything else with it. I began to feel cramped and hypocritical.

At an early celebration of the Holy Communion on a week-day morning the problem resolved itself. I had knelt down to say the familiar words of the Agnus Dei—"O Lamb of God that takest away the sins of the world, Have mercy upon us"—when it came home to me that those words, "Have mercy upon us," are the wisest and truest words that any man can ever take on his lips, that the good Lord knew all about my unworthiness and was not badly shaken by it; in fact that it was not the point at all and one had better get on with the job. I do not know how long I knelt there taking in this truth but I do recall that some-one kneeling at the rail behind me coughed discreetly and I did get on with the job.

One more illustration may be helpful. When I moved from my first parish, after sharing for six years the lives of simple, undemonstrative, and genuine people, I followed in my next cure a very gifted man and one whom I greatly admired. I have mentioned before that I made this move with considerable inner searchings and, I might add, at my bishop's strong suggestion. My first Sunday there was a sort of nightmare compounded of several elements. The old parish never looked so good, the old ties were never so strong, the old friendships never so affec-tionate. Added to that the church was packed to the doors; the new man, the first Sunday college was in session, bright autumn weather. It was awful. Fortunately I am unable to remember a word I said in the sermon but I do remember that it impressed me at the time as a feeble production. Somehow the sentry duty at the church door was survived and I went home with my family for dinner. Nobody had much to say, each one busy with his own thoughts. The telephone rang and I answered it to make my first appointment in my new parish. It was a faculty wife asking if I might see her at my early convenience. A time was set for early that afternoon and I went back to finish dinner.

At the parish office my caller introduced herself and came immediately to the point. She had been in church that morning with some of the students and what she had to say in a crisp dispassionate manner was that compared to my predecessor I did not exist. She and the students were of a common mind that I was hopelessly miscast, that I never should have come there, that the sooner I left the better it would be for all concerned, including myself. Nothing, of course, could have expressed more precisely my own thoughts at the moment. I could have improved upon Elijah; I was not only not better than my fathers, I was a great deal worse!

After that encounter I walked for hours, up one unfamiliar street and down another, busy with an inner dialogue. The late afternoon found me once more at the parish church, this time kneeling at the altar rail in silence as the sun slanted through the high windows. Finally I heard myself saying, still in silence, "Very well, God, you got me here and there must be something of some use I can do in this place. It's up to you now." Then I went home reassured—and stayed for ten years. And those ten years I would not trade for any in my life.

So it goes. The new man's newness is always measured against the old man's best and I suppose I may have done this, so to speak, to other men. The fact remains that God is good, that there is work to be done, that one's gifts however small can be used and are used. The touchstone, I think, is steadiness. There will be good times and bad, jewel-like moments of good things well done and long stretches of unexciting ordinariness, some periods of plain boredom and some painfully acute moments of knowing that one has messed things up rather badly. But through it all and in it all God reigns—sustaining, guiding, bringing good out of evil. It is enough that a man be found faithful.

After the goodness of God the fact that impresses me most is the patience of the people of God. There are always some exceptions, sometimes memorable ones, but in the large our people wait us out if we are trying at all to represent God's loving care among them. They wait for us to grow up. They remember the best about us. Time and again we are given credit for good things we did not do but might have. If we do something inept it gets around but if we do something good it gets around just as fast on that incredibly sensitive parish grapevine. The people have a certain permanence amidst the comings and goings of the clergy. They were there first and many of them will still be there when this man's place is taken by another. They know what they know and in that continuity good things can grow. In the long run I think we learn more from our people than we ever teach them. In each of the places I have been called to serve, including my present post, the people have taught me things I badly needed to know, most often without realizing that they were doing so.

A word about the succession of pastors in a settled parish. Each man makes his contribution—the net result of his credits and debits—to a larger whole, the Christian community of which he is a member. It is true but pointless to say that this man was better at so and so than that one; this is equally true of surgeons and piano tuners. The important truth is that whatever a pastor offers in honesty and willingness and patience lays down a foundation on which others can build; perhaps much better than he but perhaps, also, much worse if the foundation had not been laid. It takes many willing and skillful hands to weave a large tapestry—the tapestry of our common life in Christ. Who is to say that one part of the tapestry is more pleasing to God than another? The real question, the uncomfortable one, remains: is one's own part of the tapestry woven as well as it might be?

Now consider from the pastor's point of view the difference between one's arrival in a new parish and one's departure from an old one. As in the beginning of any adventure, the arrival has a nervousness in it. One has been looked over, listened to, investigated, and interviewed. A formal call has been issued and accepted. Now comes the venture into the unknown. Household goods are packed, good-bys are said, the move is made to a place which is nothing but a name. The streets are strange, the houses staring blankly. The stores carry unfamiliar names. The public buildings, some imposing, some melodramatic, some mean, stand their ground as friends or enemies. Who knows? The tiny group one has met from this place—are they representative? And of what, really?

And now, some years later, look at the picture. The streets are one's own streets with familiar houses and trees and sign posts. This is the street where home is and right there is the first tree to turn scarlet in the fall. In some of the stores one has come to know characters to be remembered for a lifetime and in the neighborhood people never to be forgotten. Where once were houses blankly staring are houses remembered in countless ways: sickrooms with their drawn shades and smell of medicines, shy children and noisy children whose names one remembers, kitchens where the welcome was cheery and the coffee pot always brewing, houses remembered for anguished counsels in the night, for times of desperation and fear, or for good talk, music, and laughter; and some for all of these. And to each of them goes a heartstring.

People have become persons: the old ones, glad to see a new face, retelling old memories, the teen-agers slowly or impatiently discovering "life" for the first time who will remember the new pastor the longest, the angular ones to whom one never seemed to say the right thing, the loyal ones without whom there would have been no parish at all, those who were "agin' it" whatever it was, the serene ones from whom one learned wisdom. They were all there, "the ardent, the shy, the brave." And the difficult.

And how difficult to leave! Accepting a call to a new cure is not an easy thing. It bristles with questions. How long should a man stay in one place? How does he know that he is not on the brink of some deepened usefulness in this familiar town? Whose advice should he ask or take? How will he explain to these people—his people—that he is leaving?

In the face of many sound opinions and wise words on this subject it would be fatuous for me to pretend that I have right answers to these questions. But I am bound to have an opinion and here it is. It seems to me that a pastor should go to a new parish as if it were the only place he would ever be, to embrace it, to grow up with it, to teach it and lead it and learn from it and suffer with it. Whatever he knows, including his own foolishness, can be used if it is offered and whatever he learns there can be used again. If his eye is on a distant and verdant pasture he will not do much good where he is and perhaps as little if he were to go there. People sometimes speak of a minister as "bettering himself." What a phrase!

No, a man goes to stay until he can stay no longer. And when a call to another place comes along, especially if the salary is larger, he will have to meet it with whatever honesty he has. All human motives are mixed and there is always the struggle between self-seeking and doing the will of God. But in all honesty it would be right and good for a man to leave his place—it will be a wrench at the last anyway—if after some years of ripening he feels it to be the thing to do for the best reasons he knows. At the center of this concern is a man alone—pulled on one side, urged on the other—trying to make up his mind. It is not an easy position. There are many stories about this sort of decision. You will recall the old wheeze about the invited parson who was in his study praying while his wife was upstairs packing. She could have been right, too!

I recall one such incident in my own history where my wife had the deciding vote but the stage was set differently. I was curate in an East Side parish in New York when I was spied upon by two men from Massachusetts who had come there for that purpose. They were real down Easterners—one a seasoned sea lawyer, the other an elderly hotelkeeper who looked like Mark Twain. The interview was carried on in the center aisle where they waited for me patiently and without conversation. In fact the sea lawyer after the introduction never said a word from first to last. The hotelkeeper said, "I thought your talk was all right, young man. I could hear you." And so it went with similar directness. At the end of his questions and opinions he hesitated a little then added, "Sometimes, you know, a man may not seem like much but his wife will just sort of do the trick. May we meet your wife?" He did and we moved. I can remember that old man who knew everybody in town and all about them standing at the church door Sunday after Sunday in all weathers, greeting all comers graciously as if it were the most important function of his life. Perhaps it was. Some years later I sat with him while he died. He did it well. The sea lawyer, dead now, was the church organist during my six years there. I have never had a better friend or a more helpful critic.

My lot has been cast in poor parishes, economically speaking, for which I have no regrets; quite the contrary. But it is a mistake, I think, to romanticize the "poor" parish as it is a mistake to romanticize the "important" parish. Parishes are groups of people who have bodies and souls, wills and feelings, hopes and desires. All parishes are peculiar, all are basically the same. In a good sense all parishes are important parishes. There are fine and generous and thoughtful people on both sides of any economic divide and there are shiftless ones on both sides.

The problem of ministering in different neighborhoods is one of externals rather than internals. Time schedules will differ, the proportion of people at home at any given time will differ, the amount and quality of consumer goods thought to be necessities will differ, the level of formal education and articulateness will differ, the amount of leisure time (in the slums it is known as unemployment) will differ. But internally the people do not differ; they just have different defenses. A converted man of God will be at home on any level.

Another immediate fact is the pastor's self-identification with his people, whoever they are. Very soon they become "his" people with names and circumstances of which he is a part. He is caught up in the network of their common life. This is true even in seminary when a student is serving a mission, sometimes to the detriment of his studies.

I feel that something should be said about the pastor's wife. In brief, she can be his greatest asset, humanly speaking, or his greatest hindrance. The question of the married versus the unmarried ministry has been argued for centuries and with varied results. It is urged on the one hand that a celibate pastor has more time for his ministry. He also knows the erosion of loneliness. It is urged that since the celibate is free of home ties he can more easily be at home in the families of his parish. But he has no home of his own in the normal sense to which his people may be invited. It is urged that the celibate state is a thing good in itself and more pleasing to God but I find no scriptural warrant for this point of view and more practical difficulties than otherwise. Two things need to be said, I think. If any person, man or woman, chooses the unmarried state believing in his heart that this is the will of God for him and that thereby he can serve God better, this is honest and good. But it would be unwise to say that everyone should do it this way. Secondly, the effectiveness of the married ministry depends upon the persons involved and upon the quality of the marriage, the presence or absence of emotional maturity.

The married ministry has its problems even if the man is well and happily married. We might go back a moment to a consideration of the various roles played by the minister. He inherits several austere and lonely symbols: the prophet speaking for God, the patriarch leading his people, the monk in his cell, the scholar in his study, the priest with a liturgy and an authority. On the other hand he lives in a house with his wife and children among similarly situated men, he takes his turn in driving the neighborhood children to school, he may belong to the PTA, he helps with the household chores.

He may actually have less time to devote to his ministry though this would have to be balanced against his security in being happily married and therefore probably a better use of what time he has. In general it seems to me that more of the advantages are on the side of the married ministry. As a family man the married clergyman is more accessible to other families, more understanding of their problems. He has a home into which his people may come easily. He exchanges a certain amount of freedom in comings and goings for a school of Christian living with all of its disappointments and growing pains and satisfactions.

In all this the pastor's wife can be a strength. She need not run anything to be so. Presumably this man married her because he loved her and wanted to share his life with her. In most cases she knew in advance that it would be this sort of life. But her first responsibility is to be the pastor's wife. Whatever abilities she has will be offered in their natural places. She will learn that there are confidences which her husband cannot share with her but she will also have a ministry of her own, not in competition with her husband's ministry but in complement to it. She is a person in her own right. A bishop told me that only once had he taken a new man into his diocese without first meeting his wife, and that was a mistake! The same bishop said that he considered the wives of his clergy the best Christians in the diocese.

The pastor's home is often the focus of an effective ministry in itself. How frequently are we told that modern people have a sense of not belonging and how much it means to be wanted. It seems to me that there should be at least one house in every community to which people can go for no reason at all. They do not even have to have a problem! And what more appropriate home could there be than that of the man who ministers in the name of Christ?

Years ago my wife and I moved into a rectory which had been unknown territory in the parish for almost thirty years. Certain brave souls had penetrated into the old-fashioned parlor but no farther and that rarely. On our first New Year's Day there we announced a general open house for members and friends of the parish. At first it was not believed, then the word began to get around that the report was true. On the afternoon of the scheduled day every light in the house was turned on and as people began to arrive they were asked if they would like to take their coats upstairs. They certainly would! And they were a long time coming down again but after that the house—a ten-room New England rectory—was a part of the parish life.

Some will wonder about legitimate privacy for the pastor and his family as over against the hospitable use of his house. One of the answers is an open house one night a week when people know they will be welcome. This has been going on in my house, in one place or another, for over twenty years now. It began at first in a two-room "apartment" in an old brownstone house on Lexington Avenue in New York City when a small group of young business and professional people gathered one evening

each week to talk books, ideas, theology—or just to be there.
Later on in other places it took on a different flavor; high school
boys and girls, college students, seminarians and their wives,
friends and neighbors. Sometimes the group is small, sometimes
large; one never knows. Sometimes complete strangers having
heard that they would be welcome have turned up and stayed to
become friends. The secret, if any, is to offer friendship rather
than a "program." Music, books, reading aloud occasionally,
something to eat, a fireplace perhaps—but the real point is to
enjoy one's friends because they are there.

Some time ago I was asked to talk to a group of laymen in
San Francisco on the subject of theological training. At the end
of the discussion which followed I asked them to describe for
my benefit the kind of men they thought the seminaries ought
to be turning out. A middle-aged vestryman said, "Men who will
preach the gospel and call on the people." This is the old cry
and nobody disagrees. Leaving for the moment the preaching of
the gospel, we would find general agreement among groups of
laymen, if their opinions were to be sounded, that a housegoing
pastor makes a churchgoing congregation. What are people
really saying when they use this old phrase? At the least they are
saying, "I would like some attention paid to me." At the best
they are acknowledging the fact that God has visited and
redeemed His people, that He cares what happens to them. And
how is a person to know this is true unless a man in Christ
demonstrates it again on his own feet?

Everything we do as pastors should be in terms of the reason
for which the church exists in the world. So a pastoral call is a
little missionary journey carrying the good news of salvation in
Christ wherever the people are. There are many ways of doing
this, some of them bad. In a large city hospital I have witnessed
one of the wrong ways rather flamboyantly displayed. A group
of well-intentioned ladies calling themselves (believe it or not)
"The Sunshine Visitors" made the rounds of the wards every
week or so dispensing appalling quantities of good cheer and
leaving problems in their wake to be dealt with by the over-
worked nurses. One recalls Philip Guedalla's malicious line

describing "the cheerful clatter of Sir James Barrie's cans as he went round with the milk of human kindness."

Every person in the parish should be visited at least once a year simply because he lives there. If this seems an impossibility because of the size of the parish then a real question is posed as to what a parish is. It seems to me that if there are more people than one man can know one has ceased in any real sense to have a parish. I have some idea of the difficulties implicit in this statement, and I have tried to face some of them in various times and places, but I still think it is true.

Besides calling in general there is always calling for specific cause. There are alarums and excursions in the middle of the night because someone is dying and wants the ministrations of the church. There is a family quarrel asking for a referee who may, with God's help, be a peacemaker. There are those who call this man in their various needs because he is known and trusted and because they do not know where else to turn.

By way of illustration let me suggest two examples of calling for cause—preparation for baptism and in time of sickness—then a little about making routine calling more systematic and therefore more possible.

Baptism is the covenanted means of entrance into the Christian fellowship. It is the most important event in any person's life. It is, in fact, his new life in Christ. In most cases, however, our people do not learn this fact from our normal practice in regard to the initial sacrament. It is largely our fault that baptism comes to be viewed as a social custom, conveying perhaps some vague theological validity, but mostly an occasion for a family party.

In teaching I have sometimes used a letter from an imagined friend who wants to know why his child should be baptized. The letter, a real one, follows:

Dear Tom:

It seems a long time since we ate C rations together in Korea and a lot has happened since then. I'm not such a hot letter writer but I've got a problem now I hope you can help me with.

We used to have lots of talks about things and I hear you are studying to be a minister which doesn't surprise me but it means you are the nearest thing I know to official religion.

Mary is going to have a baby next month and we want to know why the baby should be baptized. A fellow I work with says everybody should be. He says it's in the Bible. What does baptism do for a baby that doesn't get done anyway? And what's all this stuff about washing away sins? How can a baby commit sins when he hasn't had a chance yet? In the prayer book you gave me it lists promises the people have to make for the baby—like "renouncing the Devil and all his works." What's this all about? It seems superstitious to us.

I guess I was baptized once but I don't know what it ever did for me. I know you must be busy, Tom, but this all seems important to you and maybe you can tell us about it in plain words.

Yours, as ever,
Joe

The response to this letter is interesting and varied but in almost every case three points are held in common. First, one discovers in answering it that he has invoked the whole structure of the Christian faith. The being of God, the life, death, and resurrection of Christ as the means of our salvation and the nature of the Christian community are all involved here. Second is the fact of responsibility—both the responsibility of the Christian man to God and the responsibility of the Church toward the Christian individual. And in most cases "Joe" is urged to look up the nearest representative of these revealed truths, the local pastor.

When a young couple discover that their first child is on the way it means a major revolution in their thinking. The young wife usually feels fulfilled and happy while the young husband feels proud and sometimes a little threatened. Both have questions and speculations about the future. Financial matters, names for the baby, and domestic arrangements are discussed at length. What better time for the pastor to call? What better time for learning again the meaning of the gift of baptism: the gift of being grafted into the body of Christ's Church, the gift of grace, the gift of new life in Christ? How better could a pastor spend an evening in his parish? This one call may set up a whole new frame of reference for a young family—a new view of the Christian religion, a new thankfulness to God, a new involvement.

In most cases when a prebaptism call is made the question of sponsors, of godparents, comes up. Who should these people be? What do they represent? What do the promises mean? And this often leads to a second meeting, this time with the chosen godparents present, and the circle widens. I will venture to say that if a dozen such calls were made in the course of a year, carefully prepared and carefully followed, the whole quality of life in that place would begin to grow and to change.

Sick calling, whether in homes or hospitals, is a constant ingredient of the pastor's life. My intention here is simply to ask what is involved in this sort of call and perhaps to indicate part of an answer.

Sickness is a limitation. Movement is limited, freedom is limited. Pain and discomfort are limiting. One is attended by, or sometimes it seems is at the mercy of, nurses or relatives or both. The sick person does very little and most of that at the direction of someone else. He misses his familiar clothes, his view of himself. He may resent the fact that he is sick. He may have anxieties about his job, his family, the mounting expenses.

On the other hand, except in the case of a long-drawn-out sickness which creates its own pattern, an ordinary sickness is a break in the chain of habitual action and reaction. In a sense all habits are bad habits. They tend to cramp our possibilities, to make us less than we might be. After youth has passed the ordinary citizen does pretty much the same things in the same way day after day. He carries the same things in the same pockets, he follows the same route in going to work, he exchanges the same observations with the same people, he reads the same newspaper at the same time, he turns to the same form of entertainment after supper. Now this is not necessarily evil— it may even represent the security of the predictable—but it is deadening to the spirit. It often leads to boredom of which we all know our share.

Now consider this person suddenly taken sick with the chain of habitual action suspended. The doctor has called. What can the pastor bring to him other than the fact that he cared enough to come at all? Several things. He will remember that he is one of several ministers to this sick person. The doctors and nurses are ministers here whether they know it or not. There are times when the pastor will stay out of the way of a ministry which is not his own but is of God. He will remember when his time comes that he too has a specialized ministry, a particular reason for being. As in the baptism call he represents the wholeness of the Christian faith, the resources of God in Christ, carried in the person of a quite ordinary man. This does not mean that he will talk like a tract, neither does it mean that he will spend all the time talking about baseball even if the sick person is interested in baseball.

Every person has a growing edge. He may seem to be caught up in a routine which tends to reproduce itself endlessly but it was not always so. There was a time when he was curious about a number of things. There was a time when he might have done other things with his life. There are fears and regrets but there are also half-stifled hopes and dreams. There is always the possibility of a new page, a fresh chapter, a new meaning, a fresh start.

The pastor does not pry on a sick call; he does not investigate. He represents in person the compassion, the forgiveness, the goodness of the Lord. He will not make speeches about God's goodness but he will come again and again acting it out. He will plant a seed and come again to water it. He will bring different resources to different people. It will be good that he was there. When he says a prayer for the sick person it will be all of a piece with the reason for the visit. When he brings the Holy Communion it will be the whole Church in action in a little room.

One's own memories, however, are not always a comfort. Sometimes one's ministry is not wanted. Sometimes there is a wall of indifference or hostility that seems insuperable. Be patient, go to another place, but come back again remembering whose man you are. In the end gentleness is the strongest thing.

Sometimes our memories accuse us. I recall a time in my first parish when I missed one of the boys, a boy of ten or eleven, from normal activities. I made a mental note to call at the boy's home but I forgot about it. Some time later I met the boy on the street as he was delivering papers and asked him where he had been lately. He told me he was now going to a different church. When I asked him why he said, "Mr. So-and-so saw me through pneumonia." And I had not even known that he was sick!

I am sure that the heart of the matter is the pastoral relationship itself. We sometimes hear it said that the pastor was unjustly accused of not calling on a sick person when no one had bothered to tell him the person was sick. Sometimes this is true, I know. But it is also true that if the pastor calls promptly when he hears of sickness among his people that he is more likely to be kept informed. In times of crisis it makes a lot of difference whether or not the pastor has been there before.

The two temptations in routine calling are not to go at all or to call always on the same people. The only answer I know to either is some sort of system. There are pastors who divide their parishes into zones, either arbitrarily or by some natural division, and call in each by turns. Others do it by streets and roads. In any case records are essential if for no other reason than the pastor's knowing whether or not he has covered his parish. The form will vary with the individual man's needs and temperament. Some records will be simple, some elaborate; the important thing is that they are accurate and up-to-date. In a small place an older person or one partly disabled can be custodian of the parish list and do an excellent job as a major contribution.

In one parish I worked out a rather energetic system which might be worth mentioning though it would be less practicable in California, my present home, where one spends a large amount of time keeping up with new people. In a fairly stable parish of about five hundred communicants with two clergymen on the staff, we mailed cards to a number of families each week saying that they would be visited at home on a certain day and remembered by name at a weekday celebration of the Holy Communion. This was done three afternoons a week, September to June, saving the other days for hospital calling and for all the unpredictable things. It took a while to catch on but it did so with the result that church attendance increased and the parish list was kept up to date as never before. Gradually people would call in to say that they would not be home on Tuesday but would be on Wednesday and, more important, they found known calls an opportunity for saying and asking things that were really important to them. At the daily celebrations of the Holy Communion we commemorated important days for those present—birthdays, wedding anniversaries, deaths in the family. The disadvantage was that it never stopped but the parish did get thoroughly visited!

Another approach to the problem of calling is by way of categories. First calls in a new parish have a naturalness; one has come to meet the people, to learn new names and faces, and these calls have an importance since they set the feeling tone for all future calls. One learns the children's names and what their father does and frequently finds himself in the kitchen having a cup of coffee with the family and asking God's blessing on this home.

Newly married couples are another natural group for parish calling, especially when one has prepared the couple for Christian marriage and has married them. The pastor already belongs and nothing could be more appropriate than that he should visit them in the joy of their first home together, see the wedding presents in actual use, and listen to their plans. Once he has been there he has become part of their new life together and it is easier for them to call him if he is needed for any reason, good or bad.

Old people in the parish are a resource, especially for the young pastor, as well as a responsibility in the family of Christ. To the young man they may sometimes seem "contrary" but they have a right to their opinions. Frequently the young pastor goes to visit the old folks in his parish to comfort them and comes away comforted. I know of no pastoral ministry that has such rich returns for so little expenditure as the ministry to the old. One learns certain things simply by living that long. The old people's home, whatever it is called locally, is a regular port of call.

The problem of when to call on the men of the parish is sometimes discussed. Ideally one should call on a family when all are together but this is not always possible both for the family's reasons and the pastor's. I believe in calling on men where they work. The objection that men do not like to be bothered in the places where they work is, in my experience, rarely true. If a man is interested in what he is doing he is interested in having a friend of his discover what it is that interests him. Whether a man sits at a desk in an office or operates a machine or works out of doors or has a small business of his own, it is an important part of his life. Whatever is important to a man is important to his pastor.

When a new family turns up in church, and especially if there are children for the church school, the pastor will call immediately and before leaving will give the names of a neighbor or two who belong to the parish. Then he will tell the neighbors about the new people and let the Christian community work. Soon one's people will become used to spotting new arrivals and to doing something about it themselves. Once I had the good fortune to have as an active layman the man who turned on the gas in new houses for the gas company. While working in the kitchen he would find out where the people came from and whether or not they belonged to a church. If they did not or if they were our people they would find themselves being called on before they were unpacked, frequently with some willing hands to help them settle their new home.

First calls are helpful outside of the parish itself. This is the place where the pastor is to live and work and the more he comes to know about it the more effective he will be. He will call on the officials in the local government, sometimes making an appointment to do so if it is a large place. He will stop at the police and fire stations and introduce himself. He will visit the administrative people in the hospitals and he will not forget the sheriff and the jail. All of this will save time later on. He will look up the pastors of other churches. Sooner or later he will come to know a physician and a lawyer, not necessarily members of his parish, as helpful friends and trustworthy advisers. He will begin to put his roots down.

Within the parish itself the pastor will make early calls on the church leaders and on those who have known several shepherds in this place. A wise man will listen much and say little. If he hears reports to the discredit of his predecessors he will do well to remember that similar stories will be told about him after he leaves. Above all he will remember that God is already at work here and has been for some time.

TWO ✻ THE ADMINISTRATOR

If one were to pick up the telephone and call directly to the other side of the world it would not be a useful or a significant activity unless one had something worth saying when the connection was made. Conversely, if one had the most important message in the world to proclaim it would be worth while having the best possible means to transmit it. So it is with the gospel and the world. The faith to proclaim is the real concern; the means and methods of proclaiming it derive their importance from the purpose for which they are used. Adequate administration is a connecting link between the message and the world. Several of the parables of Jesus have to do with good management.

Here are some good words about the Christian message.

The Christian Religion is a religion of redemption, a gospel. It is good news, not good advice. The good news is that God, who is the source and end of the created world, is by an act of divine initiative restoring things to their true nature. In Jesus Christ, God the Son, the creative power of God pierces, purifies and transforms the creation. Redemption is always a restoration.

Thus, while the Christian Religion is primarily a gospel, it is

42

also a philosophy. This Christian philosophy contains three axioms. The first is that in the actual world things are not true to their essential nature. There has been a Fall. The second is that "the good" of anything is a recovery of its true nature, and that this recovery is made, not by any self-improvement, but by the act of God. There follows the third principle, that the true nature of any created thing is only sustained when it is held to its true end by supernatural direction and power.

The good life is therefore in the Christian Faith something to be recovered rather than created by man. It is part of his essential being. Redemption through Christ effects a recognition rather than a discovery. Man's true nature is bought back with a price.

The Christian outlook upon the nature of things as they are is opposed to that of the world. The world at its best is idealist in defining the good and Pelagian in its effort to achieve it. On its view, knowledge of the good consists in the right ideas, and the moral life is a problem of stimulating the "sluggish" will. By contrast, the Christian is a realist, he regards the good as an objective fact. It exists; it is not an ideal. It is the life of God and men in God and things in God. Men are appropriating it or rejecting it, entering the Kingdom of God or excluding themselves from it.[1]

Now we discover ~~the Reverend~~ John Doe in his office or more likely, if he is young in the ministry, in a room in his house which serves as office, study, and probably other things as well. He sits at an unimpressive desk in an unstreamlined atmosphere and contemplates without enthusiasm an ancient mimeograph. The machine sneers at him. His typewriter is neither silent nor electric. Yet here is the truth of God in the form of a letter to his people or the parish bulletin or the annual report, to be conveyed as speedily and efficiently and as clearly as possible. Here is the crux of the matter. It is a rare minister who wants to be an administrator but every minister has to be one and spends more time at it than he anticipated before the job began.

Here again we are faced with the double set of roles. The young man coming into the ministry tends to think of his function in traditional terms: pastor, priest, preacher, teacher,

servant of God. His parishioners, however, have a diffcrent set
of expectations—largely situational and functional—by which
the man is judged. Or as my former student put it, "You see
yourself as a vehicle to display and explain God's love to men;
they tend to see you as a moneymaker for the church and general
handyman."

We are confronted with another finding, that of the changing
nature of the parish in its relation to social groups. Our inherited
idea of the settled parish is post-reformation and pre-industrial
revolution. Like other social institutions it tends to harden into
a mold and to defend its right not to change. Even so, the
settled parish is still possible and workable in a small town. But
increasingly people do not live where they work; rather they
gather by association and function, in colleges, factories, hospitals, in "the organization"—that more or less benevolent despot
of the social and cultural mores of its members. In these gather-
ings are the real nerve centers. Efforts are made to meet the
changing patterns. We have come to know something of the
priest-workman movement which began in France and Germany,
the chaplains-in-industry movement in the United States, the
residential chaplain in a hospital, sometimes in a prison, who
deals with his people in functional terms. At the same time
many of these people are members of parishes in the places
where they live or at least where they sleep. Perhaps in the
future our standard ministry will be functional rather than
parochial. Meanwhile the average pastor, somewhere in the
midst of these changes and demands, has a parish to administer,
and he seems to be pulled in more directions than ever before.

We know that some ministers go to pieces and have to resign
their cures temporarily or even to leave the ministry altogether
because of the pressures on them. Part of this, I think, is the
fallacy of the overlarge parish which almost by necessity tends
to take its administrative coloring from business and industry.
Add to this the increasing demands for professional counseling
and for large educational programs and we find the pastor who
came to his ministry with a traditional and a relatively simple
set of images fighting on too many fronts and largely in un-

familiar territory. Even in small places many of us have known
the peril of trying to juggle too many balls in the air at the same
time or—to change the figure—having too many irons in the
fire, none of them very hot.

Given the fact of a traditional inheritance in a changing situation, it seems to me the root question is: What is a parish for?
Abbé Michonneau in his book *Revolution in a City Parish* asks
it this way:

What is the worth, as Christians, of this crowd that we see in
church? Do they love one another? Are they a unified element
of the community? Do they even know one another? Once out
of church, what ideas will they exchange, what influence on one
another will they have? Do they have the idea of belonging to
one and the same living Body, of being members one of another?
Has the ceremony they have just come away from united their
hearts in the one identical hope and thought? Do they go out
with the burning desire of making Christ fill their lives and of
seeing Him reign in their environment? Did they come to fulfill
an obligation for their own salvation, or did they come to
strengthen and feed a life which they want to spread? What
kind of an example are they going to be to the great mass of
indifferent souls among whom they live? Will they be a family
recognized for its charity, loyalty, faith in Christ, confidence,
joy, courage under hardship? Or will they be pretty much like
everyone else around them, except for a weekly habit common
to them? When others look at this band of the faithful, will
they have a mind to become Christians?[2]

A parish is a small exhibit of the whole Church of Christ so
that in asking for the definition of a parish one is inquiring into
the purpose of the Church in the world, viewed locally. The
answer seems to involve five live alternatives or emphases.

The parish can be construed as an ecclesiastical unit, a part
of a diocese. It has an altar, a font, a pulpit, a parish register. Its
purpose is to offer a round of liturgical activities—the sacra-
mental life of the Church—for the benefit and comfort of lay
people. Services are multiplied and elaborated, authority is firmly
established. There is nothing wrong in this, as such, but if it is

the chief emphasis it almost invariably produces the twin evils of a narrow parochialism and a separation between clergy and laity. Such a parish can be quite oblivious to the world around it. It is concerned with religion rather than with life.

Again, the parish may be looked upon as a statistical enterprise. It goes in for charts and graphs showing that there are many more people attending church than a year ago. And as for three years ago! Why, these figures are almost laughable in the face of present success. Averages are up, money is rolling in, children are flocking to expanding classrooms. At an inter-denominational meeting I recently overheard an animated conversation among three pastors each of them outdoing the others in reporting the number of children in his Sunday School as if they were scalps! The trouble with such statistics is that they can be *mere* statistics. It is quite possible to run a highly successful parish of this type and never raise a religious question.

A third alternative is the organizational beehive, the parish which is so activized, departmentalized, structured, and constantly in motion that the fast-clicking machinery seems to be an end in itself. There is a place for everybody and everybody is in it whether he likes it or not. There is no quietness here, no peace, but lots of activity. If you want to belong to a parish that knows how to make things hum, you have come to the right place! In a town where I once lived there was a local church which served meals at a tremendous clip to numerous groups and societies at work there, and apparently all the time. The figures, proudly published, on suppers and lunches served up and disposed of in the course of an active year were overwhelming. One of the oldsters of the town once remarked, "That's not a church, it's a restaurant."

Then there is the parish which views itself as a great teaching opportunity. This is nearer the mark but it can so easily become peripheral to the Church's reason for being. I think of one church I visited in a rapidly growing community where this was true to a disturbing degree. All of the educational journals were on hand. Books on adolescent psychology abounded. Books on self-improvement were bought as often as they came off the press, which is definitely often. Children in droves were taught by way of brightly illustrated booklets what people ate and drank and wore in the first Christian century in Palestine. Adult classes were advertised in three titles that I can remember: "Making the Most of Your Handicaps," "Creative Hobbies," and "Sound Church Finance." This is the absurdity of communicating ideas *about* religion or derived from it, frequently at some remove. Just as one can keep God at arm's length by knowing a lot about Him, so, by such a program, can people be inoculated against the disturbing and costly and resurrecting life in Christ.

What is left is the Church itself—what it *is*, not what some-one thinks it ought to be. A Christian parish is a small section of a faith community which is rooted in the mighty acts of God in history. It is one aspect of God's saving activity in time. It is God's business. It is the same new life, inherited in Christian baptism, which men found on the docks at Corinth when a Christ-filled man risked his life to bring it to them. In this sense it is genuinely creative. It is lawgiving because the Church exists in society. It is the continued Incarnation of our Lord Jesus Christ. It is an acting out over and over again in the spirit-filled community of the experience at Pentecost. It is under judgment, the eternal and everyday truthtelling of the living God. And it issues in a fellowship in Christ, not because it ought to but because it does. All men, all classes, all races, meet in Christ. For the fellowship is a new birth, an utter faith in God through Christ, a new creature.

Let me give you two illustrations of this faith community, this new life. One of them is from my personal experience, the other was told to me and has become common property.

During the Second World War I was busy on a sermon in my study at the church and alone at the moment when there came a knock at the door. I answered it to find a middle-aged man with iron-gray hair and a face lined with tragedy. I offered him a chair, asked him how I could help him, and waited. For several minutes he sat hunched over, his body sagging. Finally he raised his head and said quietly, "Can you give me one reason, just one, why I should not take my own life?" I asked

him if he would like to tell me something about himself and
slowly the story came out. He was a cultured person, had been
professor of modern languages at a German university. Now he
was a Hitler refugee. His wife and his two sons had been shot
by the secret police while he was concealed by friends, after
which he had made his way to America by devious means and
in great bitterness. That day he had hitchhiked ninety miles
from Boston because he had heard there was a dishwashing job
at one of the local hotels. When he applied there was no job.
It was then that he had walked the short distance to my office,
heavy-footed and exhausted. We made a pot of coffee, found
something to eat, and talked. He needed to talk. After a while
I asked him, "Why did you come here?" He replied simply,
"Your church has a cross on it. This was to be my last stop."

It was his last stop for a time. He was taken in by a German-
speaking family in the parish, members of the college faculty,
and eventually found a teaching post at a Midwestern university.
And he was restored. Mangled as it was his life began to be new
again. God is good.

The other story has to do with a man who was a respected
citizen in his city, a bank official and a vestryman in the local
parish. He was married to a charming wife, had two attractive
children. He would have been described as a successful businessman and a fine person on every count. Then to meet an emer-
gency he "borrowed" a sum of money from his bank without
the knowledge of any other person. No doubt the money could
have been raised in a more usual manner but this is the way it
happened. The man had every intention of restoring the money
and would have been able to do so except that the bank ex-
aminers arrived the next morning.

When the facts were disclosed the man's character and record
were such that the officials of the bank refused to bring charges
and even offered to make up the deficit themselves. But since
the shortage had been officially discovered the law took its
course and the man went to prison.

Some people, of course, said the usual things about having
suspected him all the time but with few exceptions the church

community closed in and took care of the family. His place on the vestry was not filled. When his time had been served the man was released early one morning to be met at the prison gates by all his fellow vestrymen who had come there for that purpose. Together they drove back to the parish church, together they received the Holy Communion, and together they sat down to breakfast. There were no speeches. That man did not have to be told about the redemptive community; he was living in it. And in the difficult days that followed he was supported in it.

Many people are indifferent to the Church because our task seems to them to be different from what it is, the offer of salvation. But if the Church has salvation to offer and does not offer it the people will look elsewhere.

Now it is quite true that the Church in the world, and therefore the parish in its community, has a number of legitimate and necessary secondary concerns. The parish has to raise money in order to exist and to serve its purpose within a money economy. It must be realistic. But sometimes I think that we give an inordinate amount of thinking to money raising. We get caught out here in trying to impress people who have money that we too are businesslike and therefore worthy of their support, whereas a true faith community would engender its own support because of the life within it. This happens, in part, in every church—the converted part of it—because this is the way converted people act.

It is appropriate for the local parish to engage in social welfare activity in its community. Christian people have a conscience, a moral responsibility, a social concern. But this too is secondary to the new life in Christ. A faith church will of necessity bring forth good works. So with the organizational management of a departmentalized enterprise. The organization is never the reason for being though a certain measure of it will be necessary to translate the reason for being into action. Similarly, few will argue the validity of good public relations though fewer perhaps will sense the loss in watering down the gospel to the level of public acceptance.

A vigorous teaching program has always been part of the

Church's life in the world. Without the spur to teach the saving truth of God, the Bible would not have been written nor would any missionary ever have left home. But the teaching is the spreading of the faith, the holy fire, the revealed truth, in terms relevant to the people's situation in time and place. A faithful Church *has* to teach.

The fact is the Church has always been a minority movement and it is a minority in every parish. In each parish there is a group of converted persons, a parish within a parish. This is the hope—this nucleus of the concerned. God is not interested, I think, in programs or budgets or in organizations or with the number of people in church, but with that fellowship of persons bound together in their new life in Christ. These are the men and women, having been "grafted into the body of Christ's religion," who accept the fact with thanksgiving, whose motives and choices from day to day are governed by that relationship. And, as St. Paul reminds us, these are the people who are at war. A seminarian, who did not stay with us, once remarked to me that he "hadn't had all these problems" before he became a Christian. This is true. The converted person is in for a fight but at the end of it—even in the midst of it—is freedom in Christ which is the only freedom there is.

Given then a pastor who has a parish to administer, and given the fact that in that parish there is a group of converted persons knowingly involved in the Christian battle and glad of it, what practical suggestions can one make? I shall attempt four.

The first is planning, and this involves more than the minister in soliloquy. When a man is called to a parish it is a good practice, I think, for him to sit down with the committee who invited him and ask them to define their terms. What is their church for? What would be missing of any importance if it should disappear overnight and never come back? What does it represent in the community and for what reasons? What *ought* it to represent there? What changes would be necessary to make this possible? Would the members of the committee be willing to see such changes made? And for the minister and his role, a similar set of questions. What do they want and expect him to do there? In most cases such inquiries make for a lively and sometimes a disturbing meeting, but it gets some place that is real. Often questions such as these never occur to us who profess and call ourselves Christians or if they have it was in the candor of childhood and we have since become insulated from asking them.

It is helpful for the members of a parish vestry or other governing body to spend a day together with the pastor, perhaps before activities are in full swing in the fall, to consider quietly and prayerfully the same basic questions. Even if there is no formal occasion where such questions are raised they are the real ones that give form and substance to our day-to-day planning.

In some places a parish council is used, made up of the heads of activities and organizations in the local church. This is sometimes helpful but ordinarily there are two difficulties. The first is getting the members of such a group to meet. The other difficulty is that it may spend much of its time in setting dates for events that have little or nothing to do with the stated purposes of the parish.

A better way of going about this, I am sure, is the device known sometimes as the functional vestry, sometimes as the vestry and commission plan of church organization. It has the initial advantage of starting with a regularly constituted and authoritative group and the added one of being elastic enough to meet the needs of any parish. The plan has both a vertical and a horizontal axis; that is, a priority list of concerns and a wide range of participation.

Here is an example of the functional vestry idea. That group of elected persons, whether men or women, spend a day together with the pastor thinking through and discussing the essential nature and function of their parish. Then they arrange their responsibilities in order of importance, for instance: worship, education, fellowship, property and finance. A member of the vestry is made chairman of each of these committees and all other members are assigned to one or another according to interest and ability. Each of these groups can be expanded then or later to take in members of the parish—according to interest and ability—who are not members of the vestry, and each group meets with its vestry chairman regularly to discuss its business.

When a vestry meets, if no thought has been given to the matter, the standard topics are finance and property, frequently viewed with some pessimism, and that may be about all. Under the functional vestry scheme the agenda of the vestry meeting follows the same priority order as in the original planning session; it begins with worship and ends with finance. Ideologically these questions are being raised: How do we go about making the worship of God in His Church meaningful and accessible to our people? How do we convey the revealed truth of God to our members as effectively as possible? What is the quality of Christian life in our parish and what can we do to improve it? As a unit of the Kingdom of God, what are our responsibilities to our community and to the world and how can we accomplish them? Is our physical condition—buildings, equipment, appointments —such as to make these things possible? What is our financial responsibility, under God, to the whole Church and to this part of it?

In my experience the result of this approach is an awakening of parish life. As over against the natural tendency of groups of people, whether inside or outside of the Church, to be divisive and defensive here is an attempt to express in action what the Church *is* and to involve more people in it for the right reasons.

The vestry and church commission plan is aimed in the same direction but is more highly organized. In one place where the plan has been in operation for almost ten years it had its beginning in a resolution:

In order fully to integrate and strengthen the work and life of Trinity Church as a family unit, and to increase to a maximum the participation of its members, be it hereby resolved that all parish organizations (present and future) become as "working committees" of the one organization—Trinity Church;— that accordingly there be only the one organizational structure (the vestry), with centralization of all funds in the parish treasury.[3]

The five commissions are worship, education, social responsibility, fellowship, and property-finance. Each of these has nine members appointed by the vestry and the membership rotates, one third being replaced annually. Including the vestrymen and certain persons with ex-officio responsibilities, this involves between sixty and seventy persons annually. In addition every member of the congregation is encouraged to regard himself as a member of any of these groups in which he has a particular interest, or of more than one, and to express his concerns.

Chairmen of the commissions are members of the vestry and new vestrymen usually are elected from among those who have taken an active part in the work of the commissions. All organizations of the parish are included in one or another of them. For example, the worship commission includes music, altar guild, ushers, and acolytes, while the social responsibility commission includes service projects in the community and ecumenical relations, both local and otherwise.

It is a matter of record that during the ten years this plan has been operating in the church referred to, attendance at all services has doubled, financial support has doubled, and many more than the usual number of people have been involved in the active life of the parish.

There will always be different and changing levels of response among people and groups regardless of official position or lack of it. Generally speaking, however, the parson might be expected to have a sense of the Church, an awareness of events and movements in history. If he is young he has a fresh view, and if he is converted he keeps it though with more realism. He has hopes. He has faith in God. Officials of the parish tend to be conservative because they have something to conserve. Naturally they think about money, about property, about the good name of the church. Usually this is a helpful thing, a balance. In one parish I inherited an old senior warden, the kind that mellows in the wood in New England, who invariably would reply to my enthusiastic proposals, "We tried that once; didn't work." On the whole that was a good thing too; experience and enthusiasm are

good influences on each other. If a man is right half the time he
has a good average.

Whatever plan is used will be important in terms of what it
seeks to accomplish, never for the successful working of the plan
itself, however impressive that may be. But without a plan time
will run out aimlessly like water in the sand.

This brings me to my next suggestion which has to do with
time and timing. Young men fresh from seminary write, "I am
finding that one of my biggest problems is allocation of time—
there is just not enough of it for even a small parish like this."
"I am overwhelmed by all the things that need doing and so
little time to do them in." "I seem almost never to stop moving
except when I am asleep and to accomplish so little. Time runs
out." Young men will find these sentiments familiar. To the
older man who has long since passed the first flush of his new
ministry the problem is a different one. His is the problem of
being his own boss and getting used to it. More than forty
years ago W. J. Carey, in his still useful book, *My Priesthood*,
described this pungently. The prose is Victorian and some of
the allusions are dated but the kernel of truth is accusing.

Perhaps the best way to become like God is to do what God
does, and our actions will react on our characters, making them
Christ-like. What then does God do? He works and He loves.
He creates and sustains the universe of heaven and earth from
the mightiest complex to the most insignificant unit. He loves
all His creation with a love that is complete and eternal.

Therefore you must work and love if you would be like God.
Ah! but is not this rather illuminating? You cannot be a saint
unless you work! unless you have some job you are doing
thoroughly, earnestly, whole-heartedly. Digging potatoes will do;
working for men's bodies will do; labour for men's souls will do.
But have you no job? Or is your work done halfheartedly, per-
functorily, unsystematically?

I verily think we clergy are in real danger here. Our next-door
neighbor, the postman, is up at 6 A.M. and ends his diurnal
tramp at 8:30 P.M. Our nodding-acquaintance, the coal-heaver,
does his eight hours' shift of transferring coal from truck to bag

or bag to cellar. But we! we are in a difficult position. Nobody can really superintend us; even in our first curacy the most martinet-like vicar can only control our external activities. Almost alone among professions our pay and position are independent of good and sustained work. The result, I venture to think, is that the hundred hardest-worked men in England are clergy; and the hundred worst slackers are clergy.[4]

Certainly it is true in the ministry that no matter what one is doing there are other things needing our attention. Often the choices seem to be in competition with each other: study *vs.* calling on the people, time for meditation *vs.* running the machinery of the parish, constant personal demands on one's time —many of these seemingly superficial or unnecessary—as over against the need for quietness and personal growth, hours spent in meetings compared with time to write sermons, and so on. How is this problem to be resolved?

As in planning, I think that a priority list is indicated here, and it will have two conditioning factors. One of them is the man's own view of what is important in his ministry (this will be largely a theological matter) while the other is a growing realization of what abilities and possibilities he himself has to offer. No man can fulfill all aspects of his ministry equally well. An effective and helpful preacher will not necessarily be a skillful administrator; a good counselor may not be a good preacher. One could make a long list of this kind. But in any case certain things *have* to be done whether brilliantly or not. The sermon will have to be written whether or not one is inspired. The resources of the Church—worship, teaching, calling, caring, listening—need to be offered whether or not one is in the mood. Gradually one discovers his own aptitudes and gifts. And if any man seems to have received little of these he may take comfort in the fact that the heart of usefulness in the ministry is not brilliance but faithfulness.

A day needs to have some structure. The old rule of mornings for meditation, study, office work, and afternoons for calling is still a good one. The secret is in getting up, even if one has been

out late the night before for a good reason. Otherwise the day
fritters away with nothing much accomplished. A short nap after
lunch (lunch should be light, I think) restores alertness, but let
it be a short one—perhaps twenty minutes or so. If one takes
off his clothes and climbs into bed, the bed always wins!

The way in which a man arranges his time will depend partly
on his own temperament. There are those who like to go to bed
early and to spring up in the dawn, full of energy, looking for
worlds to conquer. There are others for whom getting up in the
morning is not a keenly anticipated joy but who seem to grow
wider awake as the day wears on. Late sitters tend to be sus-
picious of early risers, while those who enjoy greeting the dawn
are apt to regard their midnight brethren as at least eccentric.

The trouble is that the world's clock and one's personal clock
are not always synchronized. Thomas Edison, who lived in his
laboratory much of his later life, ate when he was hungry and
slept when he was tired, day or night. This may be practical
for an inventor but it will not do for a person who lives in a
close relationship to the world around him. He is conditioned by
facts other than his own temperament. Both early risers and late
sitters have telephones. So we come back to the observation
that one of the secrets of effectiveness in a public sort of life is
to get up in the morning. One further observation: many who
habitually sit up late at night do so simply out of inertia, because
they have not got around to going to bed. And while sleep
requirements vary from person to person nobody can be consistently alert without a decent amount of it.

Another secret of good administration is the use of marginal
time. There is the story of the man who wrote a history of the
French Revolution while waiting for his wife! In any working
day there are chinks of time which either are used or lost.
Among the best uses of such moments is letter writing. One of
my clergy friends addresses an envelope and puts it in his top
desk drawer, with as much of the letter he has had time to write,
then finishes it at the next spare time and addresses another
envelope. He is seldom behind in his correspondence. The

alternative for many of us is to plan to write a lot of letters someday soon.

Letter writing even for a few minutes each day can be a pastoral act with far-reaching consequences. I can remember my delight in having an unexpected note arrive the first week I was away at college and really on my own for the first time. It was from a young minister friend of mine, not long out of seminary, but to me a personage of experience and sophistication. The real point was that he had taken the trouble to write it. I suppose he might have spent ten or fifteen minutes on it but I have never forgotten it. What we too easily lose sight of in our "larger" concerns is what such a note may mean to the receiver. People in general think of themselves as busy; a good question for many of us would be, Busy doing what?

A note from the pastor to a young couple on the first anniversary of their marriage, a note on the anniversary of a death in one of the parish families, a note to a youngster who has won an honor in school, a note to a retiring church official who has given years of service without pay, notes to godchildren on the anniversary of their baptism—who can measure these things? Again the trouble is getting around to it before it is too late. A suggestion or two here: A parish secretary can take anniversary names from the records and put them handy, with current addresses, every morning. If there is no secretary a useful contribution can be made by an older member of the parish, even a person who is bedridden, in making up such a list. A little writing two or three times a week will do it.

Another suggestion is to take a few minutes to read the home-town paper, especially if one is in a small place. The prose style may leave something to be desired but the local paper is where one will find the names of his people and what they are doing.

A day off each week is helpful. The two standard difficulties I can put in quotes. The first one is, "I can't afford to be away from my parish for a day. There is too much going on and nobody else knows all the ins and outs of it. Besides my people depend on me to be here." The word for that, as in the case of the person who thinks of himself as a great sinner, is vanity. The other is, "I guess I could take a day off all right but I wouldn't know what to do with it." That is poverty.

When a person gets to thinking of himself as a Great Man he is ridiculous (though never to himself), sometimes destructive, always tiresome. Because of the nature of the disease it is hard for the man to get over it. The man who has no idea how to use his day off is perhaps more hopeful. He is in a rut but he does not have to stay there. He needs a jolt, maybe an invitation, an occasion to see how various the world is. The possibilities are infinite. The invitation may be yours.

The same thing might be said about vacations, only more so. A time away from the customary routine (including the telephone), a time to enjoy one's family and friends in a different setting, a time to think and to plan, and the fun of coming home again. The clergyman who says, "I have not taken a vacation in X number of years," is either an egotist or a very foolish man.

I am sure that most of us go to more meetings of one kind or another than we need to, certainly more than most of us want to, but I have no ready solution to this problem. Milo Gates, who some years ago was Dean of the Cathedral of St. John the Divine in New York and who went officially to innumerable meetings, once remarked that an appropriate epitaph to be carved on his tombstone would be, "Killed in Committee." Sometimes, though, a meeting which looks in advance like being a complete waste of time turns out to be a helpful session. Unfortunately the opposite is also true. It is possible to get infected with conference-going and it is sometimes tempting to go to unnecessary meetings in order to put off the evil day when one has to do some work. On the other hand, one needs the support and the companionship of his fellow Christians and with them can occasionally make a small contribution to a larger cause. The only answer I know, insofar as I know any, is to be as judicious as possible in separating necessary meetings from unnecessary ones.

In his use of time a man works out a rhythm of his own after a while or he goes to seed. There is a lot of routine. There are many days when nothing very important seems to get done. There are flat plains of monotony. All of this is true, of course, in ways of life other than the ministry. There is the story of the Frenchman who, when asked what he did during the Reign of Terror, replied, "I survived." Sometimes that is a lot to do.

The personal rhythm is a subtle thing, compounded of self-acceptance, good humor, practical common sense and faith in God. We are all a little funny, sometimes self-defeating. God for reasons of His own puts up with us, sustains us, gives us a job to do. It is enough. In the face of that a man can spend his life trying to do sensible things consistently.

Let me introduce my third suggestion with a parable. It is a general finding in human nature that other people (whoever) cannot do things (whatever) as well as I can (whoever I am). When a man is trying unsuccessfully to unlock a door his companion knows that *he* could unlock it easily enough if this clumsy fellow would stop fumbling and give him the chance. This is often true of the administrator; he may not be unlocking the door but he hates to give up the key.

Seminarians are inclined to think of their ministry as something they will do for people rather than with them or, to put it in another phrase, clergy are better than people. But in thinking about the nature of the Christian parish we regarded it as a unit of the new life in Christ, the faith community. Given this, it follows that its life is communal, its members are members of Christ. What I am saying is that in administering a parish, delegation of responsibility is not simply a good thing to do but that, rather, it is part and parcel of the nature of the parish itself. The pastor has the privilege of offering responsibility in the name of the responsible community. He will trust his people as he hopes to be trusted. He will accept their findings. He can be wrong and will be wrong. So will his people. There is nothing remarkable in that. The fact is that they have a life to live out together, a life that grows by mutual trust.

The church staff is the representative group, the little parish, where this life in trust can most easily be evidenced. Every church, however small in membership, has a staff in effect. The members of it may not have titles or salaries but they are the little parish none the less. Someone, in the smallest place, helps with the altar, the music, the cleaning, the finances. There are the members of the church community who have already accepted responsibility before the new minister came and, very likely, would continue to do so if he were to leave. These are the people he inherits and is to live with. Older men will remember various clusters of such people in various places—some of them salty and humorous and wonderful, some of them cantankerous, some of them pale. But in any case there they were!

A large city parish is more cushiony; there are more officers, more telephones, more channels—but the people are the same people, the problems the same problems. And the administrative problem is the same, to live with the staff in such a manner that it may set the feeling tone rightly for the whole parish. A fair-minded and undefensive pastor will bring out the best in his associates. A former curate of mine wrote to me after a number of years and said he was now aware of the fact that when he was my curate he had spent quite a bit of time stumbling over his own ego. In my reply I could only say to him that years ago I had written a similar letter and that during his curacy I might have been more useful to him if I had been more grown up myself.

People enjoy doing the things they do well and we all need to be needed. If a room is to be painted or if the church basement might be reconditioned for a better use, willing hands can usually be found. We spend less imagination in other areas. A banker in the parish may be just the person to talk to the young married group about family budgets. Well-instructed lay people can be effective in giving baptismal instruction. Physicians have expert knowledge to contribute. A help both to me and to my people was a woman whose son was the first among us to be killed in action in the Second World War. She was a Christian and absorbed her loss like a Christian, quietly and realistically and in the faith. I used to take her with me when I went to call on the families of the other young men we lost and to leave her there for a while when I had gone. The people could say to me —or think it—that I had not lost my son, but they could not say that to her. It takes various interests and offerings to make a full life in a parish family. The needs and the resources are frequently in the same place unknown to each other. And a redeeming act is not less so for lack of a label.

Church music is a delegated responsibility and an important one. More often than not the church musician is not a full-time staff member and he or she is almost always underpaid. There is the possibility of a good working relationship here between pastor and choir director, one that is close to the primary reason for the church's being—the worship of God. It is encouraging that men coming out of seminary these days are increasingly knowledgeable about church music and that the average citizen has more musical discrimination than formerly. It is also true that there are more resources for the interested church musician in public libraries, phonograph records, and good summer conferences. My concern here is that the pastor and the choir director may come to know each other's point of view better, to the benefit of public worship. An hour or two together during the week, planning the music for the coming Sunday, is time well spent and often an enriching experience for both persons.

My fourth consideration for the administrator is the parish records. I became the rector of one parish where there literally were no records. My predecessor had been there a long time and explained that the records were all "in my head." Doubtless this was true but they were not in mine. In a church where I took charge one summer I encountered the opposite difficulty. The pastor left me a complete list of names with written observations on exactly what he thought of every one of them! I have already suggested that a working pastor will need accurate records for his own use; now I urge his thoughtfulness on behalf of those who will follow him there. Most church bodies have rules about this sort of thing; they are explicit enough in the Episcopal church. But no amount of regulations will necessarily lead to the desired end. A more realistic consideration is the pastor's awareness of the inner reason for the rule. This is not primarily a list of names but a list of men and women in Christ. Individuals are important to God. Souls are not saved in bundles.

It is good, I think, for a church to have a bulletin which is mailed out week by week to the members. This can be a simple mimeographed thing or a printed leaflet, but it should be readable. Its value can be considerable—a letter to the parish, a sharing of concerns, a source of information, a drawing together of the people. And in any case it means a lot of work. Most of it will probably have to be written by the pastor himself but many people can help with the preparation, addressing, stamping, and mailing. Here is another opportunity for a group of parishioners to make a valuable contribution.

Now a word about finance. Since I do not pretend to be offering a manual of directions let me suggest what seem to me the principles involved here. The parish whose first concern is the whole Church of God, the mission of the Church in the world, is the parish most likely to meet its local expenses. It may not be the pastor's job to raise money but it is his responsibility to say why it should be raised. Often it appears that the clergy are among the most generous givers to the Church's purposes. Giving depends upon conversion; one needs a motive stronger than self-interest and the best one is thanksgiving.

Finally, for this section, an observation or two about organizations. No church organization should exist except to further the purposes for which the whole Church exists. The words "club" and "church" seem to me antithetical. Natural groups lend themselves to the expression of their own interests: choir members, for instance, or the young married couples. A group of devoted women will frequently "hold the fort" in a small place against odds that would seem to be overwhelming, but women's organizations in a settled parish can become closed corporations. It is easier to start a new one than to stop an old one. In my experience a men's class is better than a men's club. Young people's societies tend to go in cycles over a period of years, depending on the size of the natural group at any given time, leadership within it and leadership of it.

The parish administrator is the same man who was ordained to be a pastor. This is one of the ways in which he fulfills his ministry.

THREE * THE PREACHER

The man of God as preacher sets out to do three things: to declare the Good News of salvation through Jesus Christ, to assist in the conversion of the faithless, and to build up the faithful.

In his useful book *The Pulpit Rediscovers Theology*, Theodore Wedel, from whom many of us have learned much, describes the individual preacher's problem sharply.

The minister sits at his study desk. Next Sunday's sermon looms. He wrestles with the "how" and the "what" of preaching. The "how" of preaching is a perennial problem, of course. The making of sermons is an art that is never perfected. Few of us are great preachers. But our problem is not chiefly technical, for a knowledge of the principles of sermon construction is not impossible to acquire. Every preacher, after a few years in the pulpit, could write his own textbook on sermon making. He has wrestled scores of times with the homiletical ritual of introduction, body, and conclusion. It is not ignorance of the form a good sermon takes that burdens his conscience as he sits at his desk. . . . No, the preacher's agony of creation has far deeper roots. He must choose a text or a theme. He must have something to say—a "message," as our elders in the ministry were

64

wont to call it. He must draw water of life for his congregation from the well of his imagination and conviction and personal faith, as well as from the Bible, the faith of the Church, and the treasure house of Christian theology.[1]

In brief, the preacher's authenticity is his own conversion. Or to state it negatively and metaphorically, *"A friend of mine in his journey has come to me and I have nothing to set before him"* (Lk. 11:6). If I do have something of the truth of God to set before my people it is because of the preached gospel which I have received. The preacher is one of a company; he learns from the Church, drawing his life and understanding from the worshiping community so that he may declare the revelation of God's saving truth, His mighty acts, as clearly as possible. Preaching is not an individual concern; it is an act of the Church.

The word for "preacher" in St. Paul's Greek text means "herald" or "runner" with the good news of salvation. This gospel, this new life in Christ, this root reason why a parish church exists in a town, is the possession of the whole Christian community. It cannot dawn on us gradually like general truth because there is no point from which it can be argued. It is revelation, and revelation of the almost incredible goodness of God in the face of the facts. For it the preacher is the spokesman, the messenger, the witness. In effect, the preacher says to his people, "Come and see what I see."

The young preacher will sometimes be concerned because he does not have more to say; having wrung himself dry he still has such a meager offering! Then he will do well to remember his real purpose in that place: to declare as much as he knows of, and as well as he can, the saving grace of God. It is tempting for all of us to preach other people's ideas secondhand, especially if they sound better than the sort of thing we usually produce. And it is pretty difficult to be original very often. But the fact is that a converted man always sounds like a converted man. He may or may not write distinguished prose but he will speak forth what he knows with a good courage and people will be drawn closer to God because of his words. The opposite—the gifted but unconverted man who talks well and engagingly about the things of God—is frightening. He may indeed help others to a knowledge which he himself does not own—such is the goodness of God—but his allegiance is demonic. The man who offers what he has, in honesty, may well discover resources which in his early preaching years he would not have believed possible.

There was a time, of course, after the Reformation and extending into the nineteenth century when sermons were standard literature. They were ornate, frequently studded with classical as well as with biblical allusions, and they went on for a long time. Preachers without the necessary accomplishments were supplied, for a price, by a flourishing group of literary hacks. The rise of the novel in England parallels the decline of the sermon as literary fare, and unquestionably to the loss of the sermon in the popular mind. Over a hundred years ago Sydney Smith—who publicized his opinion of the low estate of culture in America—wrote, "Preaching has become a by-word for a long and dull conversation of any kind; and whoever wishes to imply in any piece of writing, the absence of anything agreeable and inviting, calls it a sermon." There seems to have been no marked change during the past century; the words "preach" and "sermon" mean to the general public today just about what they did in Sydney Smith's complaint of the 1830's.

Part of this, at least until recently, is the seeming irrelevance of the preacher in a world which appears to have grown beyond his reach. In America he is not in danger of being shot or imprisoned for being a preacher; he is just not going to be listened to very much, or taken into much account in deciding important and practical things. Now we are in the midst of a Bible renaissance which has begun to change for the better both sermon writing and sermon listening. Archaeological discoveries have sparked this change, new textual knowledge has enriched it. Biblical theology is being rediscovered. There have been more new translations of the Bible in our time than in any period since the Reformation. Added to this is a new interest in symbology, a new inquiry into the mystery of communication, and the lurking disquiet that we may presently blow one another into oblivion with our new inventions.

Among other things our age has been called "post-Christian." God is optional. But there is a small suspicion in the midst of our brashness that something has been left out. "Something lost between the chicken salad and the train." A few years ago I heard an echo of this suspicion when I was driving up Vermont from Massachusetts. I had picked up a countryman who turned out to be a stonemason from Rutland who had gone down to Springfield to look up a job. We were driving through a small town which had three or four churches clustered around a common when I asked my passenger if he did not think there were altogether too many churches. Since I was in old clothes he was free to agree that this was undoubtedly true. I said I thought it would be a good thing if they all burned down and never got rebuilt. What did he think? He wasn't sure. Then the conversation went something like this. "Do you ever go to church?" "Not much. My wife goes once in a while. Sometimes I go with her to the suppers." "Why shouldn't all the churches be burned down?" Then, after a long Vermont pause, "They remind us of good things."

Another and more pointed comment on our "post-Christian" state was made by George Santayana as long ago as 1922. "Civilization is perhaps approaching one of the long winters that overtake it from time to time. Romantic Christendom . . . may be coming to an end. Such a catastrophe would be no reason for despair."[2]

As in the case of the pastor and his changing roles and the parish administrator with his problems, the Christian preacher is faced with a real situation: he still has a job to do, a body of people committed to his care, a faith to proclaim in any kind of world. Even in well-fed, complacent America.

Our population is growing faster, life expectancy is longer, our standard of living higher than ever before. More people are in college, more parents expect their children to go to college. More citizens than ever have telephones, automobiles, television sets. According to recent figures of the Institute for Social Research, Ann Arbor, Michigan, the average statistical Mr. and Mrs. Jones are 30 and 27 years old, were married four years ago in church because Mrs. Jones wanted it that way. Their salary is a little over $5000 and they will be making payments on their home, for which they paid $10,500, for the next 13 years. They have a child and a half, a five year old car, a television set, and two radios. Each of them has less spending money than before their marriage. Their average movie attendance is once every two weeks. They live moderately, pay more in annual taxes than they are able to put in the bank. Mr. Jones has about $7500 worth of life insurance for which he pays approximately $150 a year. They are healthy and they have confidence in the future.

Obviously the typical Sunday morning congregation is not made up of average Americans but they will be represented. People with names and faces and homes, old and young, vigorous and feeble, successful and beaten, mean and generous, are the given situation. They may be a roomful meeting for the first time to organize a new mission, a parish in a small town, or a settled congregation where the tapestry of their common life in Christ has been woven through good times and bad for generations. In any case they are individuals with hopes and fears and plans and souls to save. Like the preacher they are citizens, in fact, of two worlds though the secular society in which they live denies this. They are at war and their pastor, by virtue of his ordination, is an officer in their warfare. They have a right to expect that he knows the nature of the enemy, the temper of the battle, the resources to be trusted, the weapons to be used, the victory to be won. He is to lead, to interpret, to chasten if need be, to speak the truth boldly as he has come to know it in his own struggle and temptation and joy. His authority is his knowledge of God, not about God. There is a world of difference between quoting authorities and speaking with authority. The former may mean simply that a man has read a few books; the latter means that he knows himself to be a man in Christ, that he accepts the judgment of that fact, that he speaks from it because he must.

A young man facing ordination presented to his bishop the canonically required sermons. He returned after a few days to find out, if possible, what sort of impression they had made. "Will they do?" asked the young man. "Do what?" the bishop replied. If a Sunday morning production does not bring the good news of salvation for the conversion and edification of people on pilgrimage, it is not a sermon. It may be vastly entertaining, or moving, or impressive, but if it is not this man's best effort to speak the truth of God as if it were his only opportunity to do so, then it would be better left unspoken. It is dangerous to preach a sermon; it assumes so much. And dishonest sermons—like any other dishonest report—can, after a while, inoculate a group of people against hearing the truth. Strictly speaking, all men are liars and each of us wants to make a good impression. This is a fact of nature. A part of the preacher's struggle is to grow in the faith without losing his personal stamp and to grow in effectiveness without becoming proud.

The preacher's growth in the faith is not different from any other person's growth in the faith, but there are more demands upon him. All good things grow quietly and most of them grow slowly. The young preacher's self-criticism is that he has little to say, that it tends to be the same thing, and that most of the time, especially when it turns out to be better than usual, he is talking for his own benefit. All of this is true, inevitable, and not discouraging except to the young preacher. He would like to do better, and for the same old combination of motives. A greater danger comes later on when he has more to say, is more comfortable about it, and sometimes forgets who he is and why he is standing there.

In order to grow, a preacher needs regular time for reflection, meditation, and study. This does not necessarily have to be clock-bound, at the same time each day. In fact this is impossible in a public ministry. But it is necessary, and after a while will hopefully become a part of the man's own work rhythm. All people have experiences, some reflect on them. Many people read books, fewer remember what they read or even pause at the time to think about it. More people see things than notice them.

Young men a year or so out of seminary write to ask a remedy for pulpit dryness after they have run through their class notes and skimmed off the convertible parts. It is at this point, of course, that the real job of becoming a preacher begins. My suggestion is to take a book of the Bible and live with it for a year. Take one of the Gospels, for instance, or one of the great prophets, or one of the major Pauline epistles. Read it in whatever languages you have, read it in translations, study a solid commentary on it. But most of all live with it. The book will begin to unfold, the author will begin to be a person one knows. His thoughts, struggles, and convictions will take on new light. It does not follow that this book will immediately become the subject of every Sunday's sermon—better a year from then— but it will be a deepening, an enrichment for all sermons and for many other things besides. If a man were to set himself such a course and stay with it quietly over the years he could, I think, become a useful preacher this way better than any other way. We get used to the outsides of holy things. Out of inertia we become intellectually arid. In the field of biblical studies today there is enough excitement to keep any man intellectually alive. And there is the quietness of God.

About preaching "the same thing" I have two points to make. It is natural for the young preacher to do so, partly because he does not yet know as much as he will know later, and partly because a man tends to preach his own conversion. That aspect of God's truth which led him into the ministry, that point of view which seems to him all-important, that illumination which lit up for him a dark landscape—that is what he wants others to see. This is good and personally authenticated. But it is a starting place, not a stopping place. The older man who says the same thing Sunday after Sunday is apt either to be riding a personal hobby or to have given up the intellectual struggle altogether. One of the difficulties is that preachers by necessity listen to themselves most of the time and all of us are more critical of other people than of ourselves. I know one courageous parson who meets with a group of laymen in his parish every week to discuss last Sunday's sermon! It began about a year ago when an interested person—he happened to be a schoolteacher —observed to the pastor that there seemed to be a gap between what the sermon intended and what it accomplished. This was not a new thought to the preacher but it was interesting to hear it being spoken. He invited his friendly critic and anyone else who cared to come to meet with him one evening that week to discuss the problem in particular. They met and they discussed, each man trying to put the thought of the sermon in his own words, and in the process discovering both interests and difficulties he had not known before. The group averages about a dozen, not always the same people, and while it will not last indefinitely it has been helpful to everyone concerned in it.

Regarding preaching for one's own benefit, I do not know how this can be avoided, at any age, without assuming either that the preacher has achieved perfection or is without hope! He is the sinner best known to himself and he needs a lot of benefit. His insights will be shared as they come to him from his prayers, his study, from living with his people. A constant series of autobiographical notes from the pulpit is tiresome to listen to but a personal witness to the truth, slowly apprehended or newly encountered, is honest and helpful.

Many observations have been made about the temper of the times in which we live. I have made some myself. This is a perennial occupation as far back as we have written records. I say this not to belittle such observations or such interests. An alert preacher will know what is going on in the world because it is the world in which he lives and functions. He will, indeed, know as much about it as he can. But he will avoid the temptation, I hope, to settle things by calling them names. I was a member of the Lost Generation for some time before I was aware of it and when I did find it out it did not seem to make much difference. I listen to sermons occasionally that are almost all label, as if they were written entirely in capital letters. I have preached some like that myself and devoutly hope they have been forgotten. I am sure that they have been, because they said nothing. Again, there is a world of difference between having to say something and having something to say. The converted man *has* to speak; he claims our attention, our answer, our decision. And he claims it in any age, under any circumstances, in the name of God.

No preacher knows how far his sermon will reach or in what way. It is not his business to speculate about it but it is amazing, sometimes alarming, how words and phrases in a sermon will be remembered for years. I can recall sentences from three sermons, years apart, that came at important times for me. And each of them was preached by an ordinary man on an ordinary Sunday. People come with their own secret problems, their own hidden needs. It may happen that something the preacher is saying starts an independent train of thought in the listener's mind and brings the solution to a problem. It may be a familiar text with new meaning or the impact of the man himself as he struggles to say what he believes. There are down days and busy weeks and tired pastors. There are doubtless many things more important than sermons. But the gospel we have received is a preached gospel and it is ours to speak forth, whatever the results or if there seem to be none. "Take no heed of the harvest but only of proper sowing."[3]

We had a glimpse of the statistically average young American couple who have confidence in the future as a god. The picture comes out brightly colored and clear, as in a magazine advertisement. They sing as they go about their housework. But there is more to it than that. There are troubles large and small, for the Joneses and for their older and younger contemporaries. Money or the lack of it is a problem and the subject of much conversation. There are worries and frustrations, the acid of competition, the erosion of envy, the sickness of jealousy. There is the specter of the one unpardonable sin among us, fear of failure. Our divorce rate is the highest in the world, especially in the first few years of marriage. Alcoholism is on the increase, the manufacture of tranquilizing drugs a profitable business. There are wild beasts in the darkness of our civilized jungle. There is loneliness in our crowd culture.

Here is an autobiographical commentary by Artie Shaw.

Although I wasn't consciously aware of it, what I needed most in all of the world was a friend—someone I could talk to, someone with whom I could share my ideas, not only about music but about all sorts of things which were beginning to interest me. I was sick with a very common disease, one of the most prevalent diseases in our particular kind of society, a disease that is by no means confined to the music business. We are all permeated by it, and the man who doesn't suffer from this sickness is either very, very lucky or else (what is more likely) has been sick with it for so long that he has come to take his sickness for granted as a "normal" part of life.

For there is nothing on land or sea, not death or taxes, not misfortune or calamity, not disaster or catastrophe, neither thirst, nor famine, nor even unrequited love as sung by all the poets taken one by one or all in a lump—not any of these, nor any other kind of human misery I can think of—that compares with this aimless, nerve-racking restlessness, this frightful, feverishly brooding lassitude shot through with pale gleams of sickly flickering energy, this pallid, shadowy visitor who makes his home in the luke-warm vacuum of lethargy, this gaunt and hollow-eyed monstrosity called Loneliness."[4]

To some this may seem overstated but I think not. Hear another witness. This is George Tabori, a Hungarian playwright, who came to this country on a movie contract in 1949. He had observed the tide of refugees flooding across Europe, the Near East, and Africa, he had known the hell of concentration camps and understood the wanderer's sense of emotional rejection. In America he sensed what he called a "universal displacement." Here he found "everybody a refugee, fleeing from his real problems and his own reality, searching desperately for all the certitudes—economic, political, sexual security—escaping into neuroses and alcohol and sex and dreams."

One more witness. This is Margaret Widdemer's *Hymn for Grief*:

> *Luminal is what you take*
> *For heartbreak*

That is all,
Except sometimes Allonol
Or Veronal.

Prayer was used, so we hear say
In a sentimental day;
You arose from kneeling, sure
God and you'd somehow endure.

But such gestures are for us,
One would say, ridiculous,
Out of date
For the young sophisticate. . . .

"Take it with a little water,"
Says the specialist, "my daughter,
One at night and three a day
It will wash your griefs away."

Where ancestresses could pray
Slipping down a rosary
"Pity, Jesu! Help Marie!
Saints who suffered long, help me! . . ."

Now we have a drugstore god
With glass tubelets for his rod
Three along your business day,
One the hour girls used to pray.

Count them for a rosary,
Three and one: one and three:
Luminal, Allonal, Veronal.
That is all.[5]

A critical look at the list of best sellers in bookstores across the country reveals two typically consistent entries. One is the man-is-a-small-cog-in-a-large-machine novel ("even the future isn't what it used to be"). Fate always wins, individual significance is a myth. The other is the self-improvement do-it-at-home book ("the way to stop worrying is to get yourself out of the worry habit"). In this one, fate has no chance. The right-thinking individual conquers all, with peace and prosperity following in his train.

The Christian religion does not deny the problem of evil; in fact it is the power of evil that makes the Cross necessary for a loving God. There is no other way. Nor does the Christian religion pretend that salvation can be achieved by formula nor that man is the savior of man. The only real answer to fear is a person in whose company one can afford not to be afraid—like a boy walking through a haunted house accompanied by his father. The haunted house loses its terrors in the face of father's adequacy. God's answer is the Incarnation—the Person. Similarly, the only real answer to loneliness is a companionship in which one belongs, in which he is accepted and wanted because he *is*. This is the faith community. When one is brought in, loved, restored, forgiven, then he has something to give away. And in giving it away he finds himself in Christ and in community. We have not been promised prosperity or success or the absence of pain and grief, of suffering or loss. The Christian revelation is that God makes Himself known in anguish and at the thin edge of despair as well as at the wedding feast—Cana *and* Calvary.

Inadequate sermons come in several describable categories, of which the first is superficiality. James Moffatt translates Proverbs 13:17, "A careless messenger is a calamity." This is true. If the Christian preacher has the saving truth of God to offer and does not offer it the encounter is worse than if he said nothing at all. It is a calamity. Shallowness in preaching is sometimes the result of sheer laziness, sometimes an evidence of no more than a nodding acquaintance with the great doctrines of the faith, sometimes an astonishing lack of perception into the nature of the world's grief, or some of all of these. A useful sermon takes both digging out and casting into images relevant to the listeners. One's people have a right to expect that both of these have happened. A thoughtful person once said about her preacher that he spoke as if he knew some things about another country; he knew what the natives wore, a few words of their language, something about their feast days and folkways—but she was not convinced that he had ever been there.

Closely allied to superficiality is the peril of glibness. A man who has a ready flow of words, an ability to express himself easily, is always in danger of using this facility in the place of honest preparation. He knows that he can spin a yarn, turn a phrase and be entertaining. And people enjoy being entertained. This clever person is often an intellectual opportunist, making a little knowledge sound like a great deal more; a sort of homiletical sleight-of-hand. The trap here, of course, is the misuse of a gift. The same man, under judgment, can use his native ability as a vehicle for preaching that illuminates and edifies and converts. He sometimes does so, but he is always tempted not to bother. If one has "the curse of great gifts" he has a problem which most of us are able to avoid in the same sense in which most of us are able to avoid the problems that go with the possession of great wealth. But great gifts used greatly are a glory to the Lord.

Some preachers are just plain dull. The earnest man may take his preaching office seriously, he may spend hours in preparation, and still not keep his congregation entirely awake. Sometimes such sermons can be lightened by the use of pertinent illustrations or "windows," or by analogies, though the man I am describing would not easily think of them. Often he is taking himself too seriously and getting in the way of what he wants his people to see. The saving grace for this man is that he is doing a genuine job of study and preparation, and the genuineness will come through even a plodding discourse. The same person may be a magnificent pastor and preach his best sermons outside the pulpit. Many of us hope that this is true in our own case. God knows. But the preaching occasion does come and any man can grow in it.

Topicalism is a snare into which many preachers fall. One gets an idea, it need not even be a good idea—Mother's Day will do, for instance, or National Apple Week. He groups words and phrases around it, adds an illustration or two, perhaps garnishes it with a text, and behold, a sermon! This is the opposite of sitting down under a text, searching out its meaning, unfolding its implications, thinking out good ways of saying it, and offering it to the Lord.

I distrust a sermon that is full of dramatic alarms. If a preacher thumps the pulpit, strikes poses, alternately shouts and whispers, waves his arms in the air, I find it difficult to hear what he is saying. And it may be worth hearing. If a man has something good and necessary to say he would do better simply to stand up and say it. This holds true also for verbal histrionics. If a preacher chooses to declaim that, as he reads the signs of the times, the world is about to come to an end, I am unimpressed. It may be true—no one can argue it—but it would help me more to be reminded that the statement is true for me in a real and undramatic sense all the time.

One of the worst of all preaching diseases is moralism. If a preacher says to me "you *must*," I can counter this easily enough by replying mentally "Why?" or "I don't have to." The "must" in the encounter with the gospel is on the part of the hearer, not the preacher. It is the preacher's responsibility to declare the good news of salvation which convicts and converts. This is not an "ought," it is a fact. The Christian religion, in Bible and history, is not a religiously tinged ethic but a faith that speaks to us when we *can't* be good. If a preacher spends his time and mine telling me what I ought to do in order to be "good" he is not telling me news but is, in fact, only describing the real situation in which I came to church. What I need to know is that God *has* visited and redeemed His people, that there is some help for my lack of goodness, that there is a better hope than my own pitiful bootstraps. In fact, what I need to know is that the Lord of life died and rose from the dead and lives in His eternal manhood as my friend and mediator. In that declaration is my hope, my trust, my thanksgiving. And in accepting it I find the only lasting and independent dynamic for trying to live morally. Morality is a by-product of religion, not the other way around, nor are they the same thing. We love because we are loved.

The process of trying to write down, clearly and intelligibly, the thoughts that are in our minds is a difficulty which we all share. I am in complete agreement with the following statement:

My preaching almost always displeases me. For I am eager after something better, of which I often have an inward enjoyment before I set about expressing my thoughts in audible words. Then, when I have failed to utter my meaning as clearly as I conceived it, I am disappointed that my tongue is incapable of doing justice to that which is in my heart. What I myself understand I wish my hearers to understand as fully; and I feel that I am not so speaking as to effect this. The chief reason is that the conception lights up the mind in a kind of rapid flash; whereas the utterance is slow, lagging, and far unlike what it would convey.[6]

I take some comfort in the fact that these words were written by that giant of Christendom, St. Augustine. The miracle of communication is that it happens at all.

There is always a gap between insight and statement, between intention and performance. I suppose that the nearer one approaches artistry, the closer is the relationship between the truth apprehended and its expression. For most of us the gap will be a large one but it may, I think, be shortened at both ends by patience and willingness to learn. The truth of the gospel grows in one's consciousness as it is studied, meditated upon, and lived out. And the expression of it can improve both by discovering a little of how good craftsmen do it and in the development of one's own style.

In the writing of sermons there are two general approaches, from the inside out and from the outside in. In the first, one takes a text, studies it, thinks about it, unfolds it, illustrates it, applies it. In the second, one takes a theme, writes down everything that it brings to mind, references, allusions, Bible passages, finally working down to a negotiable and ordered body of material. In either case, or in an overlapping of the two, the heart of the sermon will be the truth as understood by this man and filtered through his personality. It cannot be otherwise. God makes Himself known through the people of God and the preacher is one of them. He will learn more about how to gather material, how to organize it. He will learn by trial and error what he can do pretty well or not well at all. Both of these are good pieces of knowledge. If a man has a feeling for the spoken word, for the expression of ideas that are interesting and important to people, he will begin to cultivate an attitude of relaxed alertness. He will notice, he will hear, he will remember. He will drop lines of thought into the well of his own unconscious and pull them up every once in a while to see what he has caught. He will read widely, he will be interested in everything. His horizons will stretch out and the roots of his understanding will deepen. He will have a perspective on life, a patience, an inner quietness. He will be a hard man to discourage, a good man to be with, a helpful man to listen to.

This is by way of saying that style is the man himself. There is no "right" way to make a sermon except to say that it ought to have a beginning, a middle, and an end and be as true as the writer can make it. It will be a part of its author at any given time as its author grows in wisdom. The shock that comes with the rereading of one's old sermons is in how much one missed. We learn so little so slowly but we do move, and the very fact that we can criticize our earlier works is encouraging.

There are many books on how to write sermons. They tend to cover the same ground and, in general, each one is an exposition of how the author writes his sermons. This can be useful to others, especially when the reader finds the author temperamentally congenial. But there is no such thing as an all-purpose book on sermon writing and there never will be. Similarly, published collections of sermons have the same uses and the same limitations. The reason for their being written in the first place was because the author had something to say; the usual reason for their publication is that other people thought he had done it well enough to benefit a wider audience. But, again, the vehicle of the truth is the author's style. I cannot imitate the "greats" in the history of homiletics to much purpose. Their style is not my style, their times are not my times. But I can get two things out of them. I can appreciate the felicity of their expression and perhaps parallel it a bit in my own way for my own times. Robert Louis Stevenson tells us that this is how he learned to write. Also, I can gain from published sermons the author's insight into the human situation, his knowledge of men and motives, and his understanding of the gospel answers. This is good and it is not limited by time and place and manner.

I admire a direct and simple style. It requires digestion and discipline but it is worth working at because it is the most effective way of conveying what one wants to say. Purple passages are to be avoided. The gospel message needs stating, not dressing up. Obscurity is to be avoided. I once heard a preacher describe God as the "rootless principle of the tree of existence"! A famous typographical error which found its way into print (perhaps with some collusion) is a good guide here. A passage from I Corinthians 13 was being quoted and it turned out like this: *"Though I speak with the tongues of men and of angels and have not clarity, I am become as sounding brass, or a tinkling cymbal."* Circumlocution is to be avoided. The word itself explains the difficulty! Some will recall the example of woolliness in Emperor Hirohito's attempt in 1945 to break the news gently to the Japanese people that they had lost the war: "Despite the best that has been done by everyone . . . the war situation has developed not necessarily to Japan's advantage." Sentimentalism is to be avoided. Sentiment is good and an honest part of life. It rings true. But sentimentalism is overwrought, sticky, and embarrassing. There is a good line here, by G. K. Chesterton I think: "Sentiment is jam on your bread, sentimentalism is jam on your face." A further observation on style, by an author unknown to me:

The written word should be
Clean as bone, clear as light,

Firm as stone. Two words are not
As good as one.

Perhaps the best school in which to learn directness of speech is a parish of nonliterary and matter-of-fact people. One remembers with gratitude the classic Vermont story of the two farmers at a political rally. After a windy candidate for office had been carrying on for some time one of the farmers turned to his companion and said, "What's he talking about, Jud?" To which the other son of the soil replied, "I don't know. He don't say." People who live close to the ground are unimpressed with magnificent generalities and in their simplicity often teach us things we need to know. I was walking in Vermont one summer some years ago after one of the devastating spring floods in the Connecticut River valley and fell into conversation with a farmer who had lost almost everything on which he had spent years of work. The land was washed out, timber was down, stock had disappeared. I said something to the effect that it must be heartbreaking to lose all of one's holdings in such a way. He replied simply, "We felt it." And that was all.

In my Massachusetts fishing parish I once heard by the grapevine of an exploit which seemed to me quite remarkable. Two men were dory fishing at the end of the day miles out in the Atlantic when a sudden fog cut them off from their vessel. They were too far away to be heard and they knew that their chances of finding the ship in the fog were slim. So, by wind and tide, they set themselves a course calculated to intercept the Boston-to-Halifax packet and started rowing. This was the week before Christmas and bitterly cold. So close were their calculations that some hours later the steamer almost ran them down. They were taken aboard, thawed out, returned to Boston, and were in church the next Sunday. At the church door I remarked to one of them that I thought what they had done was amazing. In a completely undemonstrative way he said, "What else would you have done?"

This is the school that winnows unnecessary adjectives out of a man's speech. Adjectives can get to be a bad habit, one that smothers meaning. The same is true of hortatory pleadings, the "let us therefores." Nothing is added in such a way and whatever has been said in straight declaration is weakened. Let a man read the parable of the Prodigal Son and be chastened.

For years discussion has gone on in knowledgeable circles as to whether sermons should be written out completely, whether one should preach from notes, or just preach. Sometimes the discussion is amusing in its weightiness with the complete manuscript pundits holding that only so can a thorough preparation be made and a finished product delivered, and the preaching-without-notes advocates insisting that only so can the relationship between preacher and people be a live one. I do not propose to settle this argument; it would be a pity to do so even if I could. But I do have an opinion about it. It seems to me a part of what I have referred to as the man's style. No one, I think, will argue that an obviously read manuscript does not tend to put a barrier between the preacher and his listeners. But a completely prepared script does not have to be obviously read and the advantage to thought and phrasing of having written it out is a real one. On the other hand, if a man can preach without manuscript, or even without notes, and do it in an orderly fashion without too much wandering he may gain in direct appeal to his people. But I see nothing heroic about it. Generally speaking, it is probably prudent for a preacher to write out his sermons completely during his formative years. He may make notes from his own manuscript later on. In practice he will probably try a number of methods until he finds the one that suits him best. Again there is no "right" way, but if one were to err it would be better to do so in the direction of too much preparation rather than too little. One finds, too, that it is a comfort to his people when the preacher has something to carry into the pulpit with him, if only a page or two of notes. It looks more as if he might have been thinking about his sermon before the time to preach it.

The preacher does not have to know everything nor to pretend to know everything. He will know what he knows, what he bets his life on, and this will be his strength. He will have an attitude of reverent agnosticism toward a number of things that he never can settle. It is possible for a man to embody an incarnation which he only partially understands. He will learn that a part of wisdom is in knowing enough to ask the real questions. Erich Fromm has some good words on this subject.

If it is true that the ability to be puzzled is the beginning of wisdom, then this truth is a sad commentary on the wisdom of modern man. Whatever the merits of our high degree of literary and universal education, we have lost the gift for being puzzled. Everything is supposed to be known—if not to ourselves then to some specialist whose business it is to know what we do not know. In fact, to be puzzled is embarrassing, a sign of intellectual inferiority. Even children are rarely surprised, or at least they try not to show that they are; and as we grow older we gradually lose the ability to be surprised. To have the right answers seems all-important; to ask the right questions is considered insignificant by comparison.[7]

Good preaching is alive because the gospel is alive. Everything the pastor does and thinks about is long-term sermon preparation. The moment at which he comes actually to write down what he plans to say on Sunday will depend upon a number of things, not least among them the other pastoral demands upon his time. Many a minister has found Saturday night staring him in the face sermonless because it has been one of those weeks. Then fortunate is the man who has listened and thought and prayed and meditated on the word of God in moments of time snatched from the clock. He will have a well within him from which to draw the water of salvation. Pastoral living and pastoral preaching are parts of the same life. I know of a man who came into the ministry in middle life without seminary training. He had been a carpenter and had thought about the ministry for a long time. But the business of writing sermons threatened him. It was not his sort of thing. Consequently, soon after being ordained, he shut himself up in a cabin in the woods and methodically wrote a batch of sermons, one for each Sunday in the year, and got it all over with forever! I have heard preachers say that they barricade themselves in their studies on a Monday morning, give warning that they are not to be disturbed, and compose the next Sunday's sermon complete from text to peroration. Presumably it lies fallow in a desk drawer all week to emerge triumphant on Sunday morning without a thought in between. This may be true, it probably is true, but one wonders a little about the feast of reason and the flow of soul being turned on and off like a spigot.

The preacher's week, on a small scale, will be what his life is like in the large. It would be a help indeed if he were to know on Monday what he hopes to talk about the following Sunday. But let it simmer a bit like soup on the back of a farm kitchen stove. So with all of the great doctrines of the faith over a period of years. A good sermon may simmer for a long time before it is fit to preach. In any particular working week the same is true in principle. If the Monday morning thought is a valid one it will keep, but it should be noted down. During the week fresh insights will be added as they occur, sometimes when one seems to be completely taken up in other duties. It is a good idea to carry a small scratch pad in one's pocket on which to jot down enough to recall the thought later on. Friday, I think, is a practical shooting distance from Sunday on which to compose the full sermon. Saturday is risky.

After a while one will have a notebook full of sermon ideas —partly developed thoughts, quotations from books or conversations that light up the mind, insights from Bible reading, questions written to oneself. It is a good idea to read with a notebook handy. Such a notebook, added to from time to time, will be the main source of the preacher's illustrations. They will be his own or will have become his own in being recognized as true. Books of sermon illustrations are pretty artificial and stories from them usually sound dragged in to fill that space. One small word of warning on illustrations. It is tempting to use recent experiences from the pastoral rounds because they are alive and fresh in the mind. Sometimes this is right and good, as a Christian witness for instance, but before the preacher quotes one of his people he should ask himself if he is free to do so, if confidence is being violated. It is surprising how easily people recognize themselves or each other even when the preacher has taken care to speak in what he thinks are hypothetical terms.

I noted, in passing, a new interest in the study of signs and symbols, by and large the only way in which human beings can communicate with one another. Several books have appeared in the field recently, useful among them, F. W. Dillistone's *Christianity and Symbolism*. Many will remember Edwyn Bevan's *Symbolism and Belief*, the Gifford Lectures of 1938, recently republished. The modern preacher will find much here to stir his imagination and increase his effectiveness. The place of preaching in relation to the totality of the Christian witness—dogmatic, liturgical, artistic, philosophical—is getting a fresh hearing. More immediate for the preacher is the growing interest in the symbolic meaning of words themselves, the study of semantics. The man who attempts to convey the truth of God by way of the spoken word is constantly faced with the problem of translation. Some years ago in a college parish I received a small delegation of interested students who gave me an assignment. They had listed several classical words of the Christian faith—Sin, Grace, Judgment, Salvation, Redemption, Forgiveness—and asked, "What do these words mean in American?" We spent a good part of a school year together trying to find out. I hope it was as much help to them as it was to me.

It has been pointed out, and justly so, that the person listening to a sermon has the right, under God, to reject the preacher's statement. Represented in any congregation are various levels of ability to listen and various levels of Christian maturity. Between preacher and people there is actually a dialogue though it may not appear to be so. If a person is not free to say "No" he is never free to say "Yes." In a sense preachers are made by their listeners.

Preaching is always pastoral. It is not simply a declaration, it is a declaration to these people. I sometimes wonder how much good is accomplished in our curious custom of multiplying sermons during Lent, preached mostly by visitors not to be seen again for another year. More important, I am sure, is to take the pastoral concern of preaching to that large part of the world which is not found in church. There seems to be an opening here in natural groups. I do not mean the usual clubs and societies who need a speaker for a "program," but labor unions, business and professional groups who invite the minister to speak to them, not so much to be entertained as to hear what he has to say about their concerns. The Church has a mission to all people, not only to those who gather in churches on Sunday mornings but to those in factories and schools, in slums and prisons and in the dark places of our society.

The spoken word is at the center of our witness, the good news embodied, the faith proclaimed.

FOUR ❋ THE TEACHER

In a piece called "The Dogma is the Drama," published in America by *The Church Review* in 1942, Dorothy Sayers included a questionnaire on the Christian faith with contemporary answers.

She says:

Judging by what my young friends tell me, and also by what is said on the subject in anti-Christian literature written by people who ought to have taken a little trouble to find out what they are attacking before attacking it, I have come to the conclusion that a short examination paper on the Christian religion might be very generally answered as follows:

Q. What does the Church think of God the Father?

A. He is omnipotent and holy. He created the world and imposed on man conditions impossible of fulfillment; He is very angry if these are not carried out. He sometimes interferes by means of arbitrary judgments and miracles, distributed with a good deal of favoritism. He likes to be truckled to and is always ready to pounce on anybody who trips up over a difficulty in the Law, or is having a bit of fun. He is rather like a Dictator, only larger and more arbitrary.

Q. What does the Church think of God the Son?

A. He is in some way to be identified with Jesus of Nazareth. It was not His fault that the world was made like this, and, unlike God the Father, He is friendly to man and did His best to reconcile man to God (see atonement). He has a good deal of influence with God, and if you want anything done, it is best to apply to Him.

Q. What does the Church think of God the Holy Ghost?

A. I don't know exactly. He was never seen or heard of till Whitsunday. There is a sin against Him which damns you forever, but nobody knows what it is.

Q. What is the doctrine of the Trinity?

A. "The Father incomprehensible, the Son incomprehensible, and the whole thing incomprehensible." Something put in by theologians to make it more difficult—nothing to do with daily life or ethics. . . .

Q. What does the Church think of sex?

A. God made it necessary to the machinery of the world, and tolerates it, provided the parties (a) are married and (b) get no pleasure out of it.

Q. What does the Church call Sin?

A. Sex (otherwise than as exception above); getting drunk; saying "damn"; murder, and cruelty to dumb animals; not going to church; most kinds of amusement. "Original sin" means that anything we enjoy doing is wrong.

Q. What is faith?

A. Resolutely shutting your eyes to scientific fact.

Q. What is the human intellect?

A. A barrier to faith.

Q. What are the seven Christian virtues?

A. Respectability; childishness; mental timidity; dullness; sentimentality; censoriousness and depression of spirit.

Q. Wilt thou be baptized in this faith?

A. Not by a long shot!

I cannot help feeling that as a statement of Christian orthodoxy, these replies are inadequate, if not misleading. But I also cannot help feeling that they do fairly accurately represent what many people take Christian orthodoxy to be, and for this state of affairs I am inclined to blame the orthodox. Whenever an average Christian is represented in a novel or a play, he is pretty sure to be shown practising one or all of the Seven Deadly

Virtues enumerated above, and I am afraid that this is the impression made by the average Christian upon the world at large.

It is the dogma that is the drama—not beautiful phrases, nor comforting sentiments, nor vague aspirations to loving-kindness and uplift, not the promise of something nice after death—but the terrifying assertion that the same God Who made the world lived in the world and passed through the grave and gate of death. Show that to the heathen, and they may not believe it; but at least they may realize that here is something that a man might be glad to believe.[1]

Christians have inherited a body of revealed data, a world view, a basis for criticism, a faith. But often in history the Church as an institution has spent a great deal of energy in protecting a privileged position, labeling any opposition as irreligious or worse. Often the Church instead of leading the world follows it, eagerly putting the rubber stamp of respectable approval on the world's values, especially when they seem to be successful. What is apt to emerge in the view of fair-minded and uncommitted people is a picture of official Christianity as dull, disapproving, and defensive. The charge is sometimes deserved. The Church did, for instance, try to stifle the Copernican revolution in the face of the facts, and ever since the time of Constantine, when the Church became official and church-going expedient, individual Christians have had to contend against respectability.

More immediately, various facts of the religious history of America are discernible and influential in the culture pattern. The political and religious upheavals of sixteenth- and seventeenth-century Europe were evidenced in America both in the multiplicity of religious groups and in the bitterness among them. Religious toleration has been and still is a slow growth. In the eighteenth century the Great Awakening, a romantic movement appealing to individual piety and emotional response, was balanced by the Enlightenment, an intellectual and scientific movement appealing to a desire to be rid of traditional institutions and fostering a belief in the unlimited perfectibility of man. The next century saw the decline of interest in dogma and the rise of the temperance and slavery issues, the beginnings of the capital-labor trouble as a moral problem. It is difficult for Americans to see their more immediate past in perspective—big business, the settlement house movement, the "social gospel," prohibition, boom and depression and war, a parade of personal gospels, the advent of the atomic age, of new and bigger foxholes.

A blend of these movements is to be found in the current temper of America. We are a warmhearted people tending to support causes and to be moralistic about the rest of the world. We have reached a high level of scientific inquiry and achievement. But we are also largely anti-intellectual, afraid of ideas and of controversy. To quote Santayana again, "American life is a powerful solvent. It seems to neutralize every intellectual element, however tough and alien it may be, and to fuse it in the native good-will, complacency, thoughtlessness, and optimism."[2] Underneath this trademark sort of optimism our anxieties flourish, our peace of mind cults become a business. What this all adds up to for the average citizen is a mixture of hope and futility and a suspicion that no real answers are to be found anywhere.

In a previous section I mentioned the Bible renaissance of our times. This is the major element left out of the last paragraph and, in my opinion, most hopeful for the Christian teacher. Here as a result of what came to be called, perhaps unfortunately, the "higher criticism" is a workable combination to our good, of scientific inquiry and personal commitment to the truth of God. The process of enlarging our mental and propositional horizons is sometimes a painful one—something like putting a picture window in the old homestead—but the view is better and there is more light inside.

Let me offer a simple illustration. A bright and inquiring twelve-year-old decided not to be confirmed at the usual time. This on two grounds: first, as she experienced it there seemed to be a mistiness in Church doctrine as over against the positive colors of the world; secondly, there seemed to be a scarcity of evidence for the Church's alleged facts. Her parents were interested and untroubled, suggested that she take a year or so to think about it. The child accepted the reprieve and continued to inquire. One Sunday, having heard in church the story of the feeding of the four thousand (Mk. 8:1–9) she remarked, "You know, some other fellow in the Bible told the same story but he said there were *five* thousand. Did he tell it second?" This led to looking up the references (there are eight of them) and to a simple exposition of the Synoptic Problem. At the end of it the girl said, "This is interesting. Why don't they tell us about these things in Sunday School instead of making believe there isn't any problem?" A fair question and a bothersome one for a pastor faced with the selection and training of teachers. But for the child it was a first encounter with actual Bible *study*, and it was illuminating. What came out of it was the question of why the story was told and recorded in the first place—a better question than the conflicting mathematics with which she started.

I think it is wise for us to remember that this attitude toward the study of the Bible and its findings is pretty new, though its "newness" will vary from place to place and from group to group. The spirit of inquiry, typical of the Enlightenment, which gained impetus from Lessing's book in 1784, *A New Hypothesis concerning the Evangelists, considered as purely Human Writers of History*, led to a new view of the authorship of the Pentateuch and to the solving of the Synoptic Problem. For many of us this point of view is welcome, creative, and truth-serving but to many others it is still a threat. There are vigorous rumblings, even now, about the Science *vs.* Religion controversy though Darwin's *Origin of Species* was published almost exactly a century ago. The point still sometimes needs to be made that the reason for any study of the Bible is twofold: to discover as objectively as possible what is being said, and to discover its meaning for us.

Many honest religious questions are never raised, especially by adults, because the proper time and place in which to raise them do not seem to occur, or because one does not wish to expose his ignorance, or because one senses that such an inquiry would appear to be disrespectful or irreligious. As a result many intelligent people drift away from the Church or remain outside.

The fault is largely our own. We have been enjoined to love the Lord with all our mind. It is our responsibility to know the tools of inquiry and with their help to lead our people into a deeper and tougher and livelier faith.

This does not mean that the minister has to do it all himself but it does mean that he needs to be aware of the problem and the resources, and to provide the leadership. He may start a Bible study group with no more than half a dozen interested people and find that a year later he has provided leadership for six other groups. I am sure about two things here. One is that the actual stuff of Bible study—texts, versions, commentaries, geographies—is interesting to any normally intelligent person, and leads him closer to God. The other is that something good happens in and through a small group which meets for such a purpose. The small group has a genius of its own which is quite different in character from that of a large group or from the experience of two people meeting together.

A Bible study group can be set up in a number of ways. There are many helpful books here. In my experience I have found it workable to tackle a single book or a part of a book at a time, and to have each person in the group responsible for the point of view of a version or commentary, or some aspect of the study. These assignments can be changed from time to time but the responsibility itself increases interest especially when points of view are in conflict and the group has to do some digging to see where they think the truth is. This can be a very exciting business and I have never known it to decrease a person's faith; quite the contrary. It is healthy for a parish to have a number of small groups meeting consistently and inquiring into the sources of the faith. And, once this begins, it is fascinating to see unsuspected leadership produce itself from the parish ranks.

In the Gospels Jesus is commonly addressed as Teacher, not only because He was looked upon as standing in the rabbinical tradition but because He taught constantly and clearly, though often disturbingly. He was self-authenticating. He spoke with authority and not as the scribes. He was at the center of whatever concerned people most: birth and death, making a living and politics, marriage and children and families, getting along with one's neighbors, pride and forgiveness and anxiety and eternal life. He was in all of them, listening, teaching, interpreting. Simple questions were answered simply, trick questions meant to embarrass Him were given back on a different level. The great questions which have always interested mankind He illuminated in analogies or parables, illustrations in depth of human nature and God's response to it. After one of the hard sayings when many of the half-interested left Him He asked the disciples, "Will ye also go away?" Peter replied, *"To whom shall we go? thou hast the words of eternal life"* (John 6:67, 68). So the Christian teacher. There is a story about a not very large young priest who after preaching one Sunday was being browbeaten at the church door by an angry and imposing woman. "You are a very young man," she said, "to be talking like that." The young man drew himself up as tall as possible and replied, "Madam, I represent eternity!" He was, of course, speaking the precise truth though there are various ways of doing it. The Christian teacher represents nothing less. Christian education is Christ.

The parish itself is a teacher, of one thing or another, all the time. A few years ago when the Episcopal church was gathering background data for a new approach to Christian education I was struck by some findings on the attitudes and information of average twelve-year-olds in average parishes across the country. Here they are in summary form.

God is large, powerful, vague, judgmental. Jesus Christ is associated with Christmas, His birthday. This is a good time for our reporters, involving gifts, family celebrations, a general feeling of good will. Christmas carols get a plus mark. Other than that Jesus performed miracles, most of them puzzling, and had disciples. He told parables, the most memorable ones being those with the most action, notably the Good Samaritan. Jesus was condemned and put to death in a brutal manner (this is puzzling) and on Easter is said to have risen to life again (also puzzling). They know something about life in Bible times and remember the names of some Bible characters, especially people of action. The best-known Old Testament figure is David who did heroic deeds when he too was young.

The church is large, dark, has a characteristic musty odor and a screechy choir. The church is full of irrelevant people for whom children seem to be a nuisance. Boys know that there are activities of an official nature with which they may be associated; girls have less expectation of any such thing. They all know that the church asks for money and they are involved financially in a small way. They know that the church supports missionary activity, usually in some faraway place.

The average twelve-year-old will have prayed in his own emergencies, for the most part petition and intercession. He will know that other people pray. His own prayer life or system will depend on the practice of his own family. If he is taught to pray at church and observes that his parents do not do so he soon gives it up as not worth while. He will know parts of the services of the church unconsciously—words, phrases, names. He has a strong and specific sense of right and wrong. Injustice on his own level bothers him very much. He has a strong sense of belonging or not belonging in his ordinary life; this is not as strongly felt in his church connection. He will have seen a baptism, a wedding. Death means grief and a sense of personal loss if the person is known and loved. The death of old people seems natural. On the whole the Church appears to be against fun and religion means being good.

We are faced here with the same gap described by Dorothy Sayers, the gap between what the Christian faith is and the impression given of it by Christian people. We teach all the time, knowingly or unknowingly. It has been observed that the most effective educational device in the world is the conversation which children overhear in their own homes. This is just as true of the local church. Add to that the building itself, attitudes spoken and unspoken, the fact that the equipment is not as good as that in the secular world, the colors not as bright, the issues (as usually presented) not as immediate—and one begins to get some idea of the power of the teaching that is going on constantly. On the positive side one good teacher with imagination and perception, using any sort of setting and equipment, can change lives.

The average parson in the average parish is a man of good will. He has a sense of responsibility for conveying the truths of the faith in meaningful ways. He thinks about this every time he prepares a sermon. But he often finds it difficult to see and to plan a teaching program in the whole parish, with all of its levels and changes and confusions. There are never enough good teachers. There is never enough time. It all seems so ineffective.

This moment of panic happens not only to the young minister in his first parish but to many a pastor facing a new September with school about to begin. Then, hopefully, he will remember that the place to start is not at the nearest source of lesson materials but with the heart of the parish itself, the faith community. Long ago someone said that the Christian faith is not taught so much as it is caught—but that *is* teaching! The group of converted, thankful people teach all the time, too. These are the people who have something to give away. Let the pastor meet with them and share his concerns and soon parents will be curious, then interested, then involved. Teachers will come out of them; a group interested in the whole educational structure of the parish will come out of them, and religious education will have begun. It is not a department, not an "activity." It is a parish family of all ages alive in the Lord.

It will need representative persons just as the pastor himself is a representative person. It may be that the parish is able to employ a trained director of Christian education and if so it will be a cause for thanksgiving. This is a new ministry in our times and a useful one. More and more women are finding in this profession a combination of major interest and livelihood. Training schools and seminaries are unable to supply the demand for them. Here is a staff member, a colleague to be welcomed and listened to and used.

Teachers in our parish educational program should be the most mature and free Christians who can be found. If this concern has a priority for the pastor that fact will communicate itself. The teachers themselves will want to be trained and the minister will again find himself a teacher of teachers. A parents' class not only increases the effectiveness of the children's Christian education in a co-operative understanding but also makes it possible for adults to learn about their faith facts which they have never had an opportunity to learn before.

A parish library can be a useful resource but not if it is a graveyard of unloved, unreadable, and ancient derelicts or a bright twitter of success books. It need not be large but it does need to be well selected and vigorously pruned from time to time. This means that a qualified person is in charge. Book buying should be a budget item, and some imagination spent on the location and use of the library. A number of good books for such a library are now in paper backs.

Many observers believe that the Sunday School as an institution has had its day. This is certainly true of departmentalized activity "for the children." When classes for various age groups can best meet is a subject to be discussed and decided locally. In some places the whole formal educational structure has been moved to Saturday with good results, not the least of these being increased time. Many churches have high school and adult classes on weekday evenings. These are details. Central to any other consideration is the Church at worship, the characteristic activity of the Christian family, the glad response to the love of God. Out of that comes Christian education.

The two poles for the Christian teacher are truth and relevance. For some time in a college parish I kept a record of the religious questions raised by students when they really wanted to know the answers. I stopped after a while because they were always the same questions, occasionally with a different twist. They were the same questions I had asked, the same ones which have classic statement in the Bible. In short, they were the real questions. The parents of these students have the same inquiries but unless they are in an accepting group they are less willing to ask them. The questions, each of them actually a series of related ones, are these.

1. What is the evidence, if any, for the existence of a personal

God who is just and loving? How did He come to create the universe in the first place? And if He did so, why is there evil in it? Assuming that a just and loving God exists, what evidence is there that He cares about me? A personal Incarnation seems impossibly extravagant.

2. What is the evidence, if any, for survival of human personality after the death of the body? Is such a survival desirable? What is personality anyway? What is the difference between time and eternity? What is heaven? What is hell? Is there an intermediate stage and, if so, is one free to make choices in it?

3. What is sin? How can the death of Christ two thousand years ago have any effect on my sins, supposing that there is such a thing? Did Jesus Christ actually rise from the dead and, if so, what difference does it make to me? Why is the Church so preoccupied with sexual morality?

4. What is the nature of the Church? Is it a human institution or a divine organism? If the latter, why is it divided? Did the Church make the Bible or did the Bible make the Church? What is the authority of the Bible in the light of modern criticism?

5. Are the traditional Sacraments valid today or were they simply a part of a medieval world view? Does baptism actually *do* anything to a person? What actually happens in the Holy Communion?

6. How do I know that God listens to my prayers? What if I don't want to pray at all? What if I pray and nothing happens? Why should I tell God things He already knows if He is God? What if I try to pray and have no sense of communion with God?

I remember the first study group I ever tried in a parish of my own. It was a dismal failure. The good wives were willing enough to have me carry on during Lent at their regular Thursday meeting if I really wanted to. They thought I was a nice young man and doubtless meant them well. But it ended where it began. The subject matter was not very interesting to me—a mission study course for Lent—and I made it about as relevant as the mountains of the moon. Once again, the trouble with an experience of this kind is that teaching goes on. It says, in effect, that the Church is interested only in things that do not matter much one way or another and that religion is dull. This is the opinion of much of the world outside the Church. But the real questions are still there, disturbing and insistent, waiting to be asked.

The good teacher has three qualities. First of all he knows something; he owns it. He is converted. He has convictions. Secondly, the good teacher is a person of perception. He sees into the matter of the teaching. He sees what it says, what it means, what it implies. There is an interesting story about the Swiss biologist Louis Agassiz who was a distinguished teacher at Harvard some years ago. A young and eager graduate student was assigned to the old scholar and congratulated himself on his good fortune. On the first morning of the new partnership Agassiz gave the young man a small object in a fold of paper, asked him to take it back to his own laboratory and identify it. The student was back in no time to say that it was a scale of a fish, implying by his manner that one need not have achieved the status of graduate student to identify such things. Agassiz, unperturbed, sent him back to look at it again. When he returned some time later the student had a lot more information —what sort of fish, its approximate age, the place from which the scale was taken. This process went on, the young man turning up more data and the old man sending him back, until the student came to perceive that in that fish scale he was look-ing at a perfect example of functional design, a thing of beauty in itself, a witness to millions of years of the developing process of nature, a thing of wonder. Only then was he ready to begin to learn. Years later the graduate student, then a teacher him-self, spoke of this incident in his personal history as "how Agassiz taught me to see."

The third quality of the good teacher is a willingness and ability to translate. However deep the conviction, however keen the perception, a bridge is needed between minds, a sort of Rosetta stone, making it possible for one to reach the other with meaning. In His teaching Jesus translated eternal truths into the language of simple people in a rural setting. His genius is such that these analogies are universals. They are stories of

Everyman, on journey. At first hearing, what seems to be the account of a rustic incident—almost a piece of journalism—turns out to be a searching of our motives and a revelation of the nature of God. In the picture the listener finds himself and judgment and grace.

Just as Jesus took His illustrations from the world in which He lived so the Christian teacher today learns from the world around him and uses it as a vehicle for his teaching. Christian people have often shown a reluctance to learning from the world, at times going so far as to describe the world which God made as evil in itself. That this is a heresy and so declared by the Church has not prevented this confusion from plaguing us. Long after his conversion from "the world" St. Augustine wrote, "Whatever is true, by whomsoever it is spoken, proceeds from the spirit of God."

Among the wisest commentators in any age are its humorists. They are among the seers. We enjoy the sanity of Mark Twain and Will Rogers, of James Thurber and E. B. White. In one of his *Further Fables for Our Time*, Thurber tells a story of an old ostrich instructing a class of young ostriches in their own excellences. A skeptic named Oliver says, "Man can fly sitting down, and we can't fly at all." To which the old ostrich replies witheringly, "Man is flying too fast for a world that is round. Soon he will catch up with himself, in a great rear-end collision, and Man will never know that what hit Man from behind was Man."[3] Some of the best writing and some of the sharpest criticism of our times is to be found in "Notes and Comment" in *The New Yorker*. And for a disturbing piece of insight I commend E. B. White's Air-raid Drill in *The Second Tree from the Corner*. The truth is where you find it and it is all God's truth, the wind of the Spirit.

A number of theological seminaries have courses where some examination is made of the world's mind as expressed in literature. In the seminary where I teach such a course is offered. Top best sellers, standard works which are reprinted and reread, and currently popular plays are the required reading and three groups of questions are asked about each book. First, why do people read this book, or why does it remain popular, or why do people recommend this play to their friends? What need does it meet? Secondly, what precisely does the author say? What are his presuppositions? What do his characters believe in? What is his idea of success? Thirdly, what are the theological implications of his position? Where would it take you? This approach has led to some lively discussions; it has demonstrated that there are good things to be learned from the world. It has helped students to think in relevant terms. The difficult question, of course, is the second one: What does the author say? We would prefer him to say the things with which we already agree or against which we have a ready answer. In order to deal truthfully with ideas not so easily disposed of one has to learn to listen carefully, to weigh evidence fairly, and to resist thinking in terms of labels. A venture of this kind can be tried by any group of people.

The Christian teacher is faced with the fact that church people often exhibit two quite different negative tendencies. One is to retreat from the world, almost to hide from it, in an uncritical sort of churchiness. The other is to present in daily living a set of values indistinguishable from those of the world. I remarked this earlier regarding the minister himself; it is equally just of church people in general. The Christian teacher does not confuse the whole of the faith with his own understanding of it. He knows that to be humble means to be objective. He will remember the symbol of the Centurion on Calvary, the uncommitted professional soldier, who makes observations and draws conclusions. He will remember the skeptical Nathaniel asking if anything good can come out of Nazareth and he will be concerned about honest reactions when the skeptic comes to see. The Christian revelation, the fact of Christ, either is the key to all of history or it is simply one of many events in the long unfolding of the human story. I choose the former by an act of faith but I cannot persuade my neighbor, a geologist, to accept it unless he sees some value in it as evidenced in my life, and unless I can explain it in terms that he can accept. "*Go ye therefore, and teach* . . ." (Matt. 28:19).

We sometimes look back longingly to the medieval synthesis of arts and sciences under the aegis of the Church. Insofar as such a synthesis existed it was the product of a theological outlook which embraced the whole of life, and is just as true now as then. But the world has changed considerably. There was a time when one highly intelligent person could contain within his own mind practically all known facts. The European world was a small place with a small cosmology. Now we grope for a synthesis of any kind. Knowledge is enormous and diversified, our cosmology expands daily. It is estimated that our factual knowledge doubles every ten years. In the midst of all this, however, the truth remains that Christ is the focal point of history, and that the whole of life is to be redeemed. The Christian teacher will be alive to movements and developments in art and architecture, music and drama, poetry and medicine and physics —not only because they are interesting aspects of an immensely variegated world but because they are activities of people for whom Christ died and rose from the dead and for whom He lives to fill all things with meaning. The Christian teacher will go with a good courage, knowing what he knows, but with a ready eye and a ready ear for expressions of the truth of God other than his own. All knowledge, whether that of a child or a nuclear physicist, begins with wonder. The wonder of the child, who is a natural metaphysician, and of his laboratory-trained parent leads to an inquiry into the nature and destiny of man under God. This is theology.

Future historians, I think, will note as one of the marks of our century the drawing together of Christian bodies split at the time of the Reformation and since then. This has come to be known as the ecumenical movement. The word "ecumenical" alludes to a theological fact, that the Church is one, and indicates a hope that this may become visibly true in the world. It is an ancient Greek word meaning "from or for the whole inhabited world," but its too easy use sometimes gets us into difficulties by assuming too much. There are divisions over real theological issues, there are vast temperamental differences within the Christian family, there are important historical divergences along the way. None of these can be wished away. On the other hand, the Church of Christ *is* one Church and from this fact the ecumenical concern of the Christian derives.

My thoughts on this subject come under the heading of Teacher because the Church itself, the whole Body of Christ, the holy fellowship, is our teacher. Assuming, as I shall, that the disunity of Christendom is a sin and that no existing ecclesiastical body contains in itself the fullness of the Christian faith, I have four observations to make. The first is that the person who has enough knowledge of the Christian body to which he belongs to be secure in it has something to share with other Christians and is free to do so. After I had been pastor of a church for several years in a New England city I was invited to preside over an interesting experiment. Six local churches, my own included, had been asked to choose three men apiece to meet together on six Sunday evenings for an inquiry into their Christian heritage. Each group in turn was to speak briefly about the history, doctrine, discipline, and worship of its own tradition and to lead the discussion which followed. I was the only clergyman present, my function being to define terms and to keep the discussion on the point. Besides a relaxing of defenses and a general sharing of information two things stood out in those meetings. One was that the men who knew the most about their own church groups had the most to offer not only in facts but in understanding as well. The other was that at the end of the six weeks there was a consensus on some of the fundamentals of the Christian faith and a clearer view of important differences. There also was a growth in charity.

My second observation is that we have good things to learn from one another not only in point of fact but also in terms of emphasis. To us who stand in a liturgical tradition the "free" churches have something to say about personal witness and about the ministry of the word. Liturgical churchmen have a contribution to make in terms of a continuing tradition of prayer and praise and of forms of worship in which centuries of Christians have found themselves at home. Archbishop Temple, a secure Anglican, said in 1944:

In our dealings with one another let us be more eager to understand those who differ from us than either to refute them or to press upon them our own tradition. Our whole manner of speech and conduct, and of course supremely our mode of worship, will inevitably give expression to our own tradition. Wherever there are divisions there is sure to be something of value on both sides. We ought always to be eager to learn the truth which others possess in fuller degree than ourselves, and to learn why some give to various elements in our common belief a greater emphasis than we are accustomed to give. Our temper in conference must be rather that of learners than that of champions.[4]

Thirdly, the series of international and interchurch conferences which have marked this century has defined real issues and real differences with a vigor and clarity which may hasten their resolution. At no time in the preceding three centuries has there been such an approximation among the theologians of all Christian Communions, such a sharing of thoughts and insights, such a knowledge of points of view.

Fourthly, "nothing is real until it is local." It is possible for the leaders of Christendom to meet, discuss and resolve, and to have the local church situation as little affected as if the meeting had not taken place. One of the difficulties is, of course, that in the local situation there are various factors which are sociological as well as theological. Human nature takes over and the high-level conference might just as well have met on Mars. There are practical things that can be done about this if there is a will to do so. One is the small group with several church bodies represented, meeting together to share what they believe and what they hold in common. We tend to dislike people, or at least to distrust them, categorically. It is easier to like people with whom one has shared thoughts and convictions and to discover in doing so why these thoughts and convictions are important.

Another fruitful enterprise is for the minister to study a book of the Bible with another pastor in his own town. One soon discovers a congenial person and, very likely, he has had some such plan himself but never got around to doing much about it. Let these two men spend some time together once a week during the winter reading, say, the Epistle to the Ephesians, or St. Mark, and they will have gained not only in textual knowledge but will have exchanged many points of view to their mutual advantage.

There are three sorts of ministerial fellowship each of which can be a learning experience for the pastor as teacher. There is the general gathering of pastors of one church body in an area —the diocesan clergy, for example. It is a necessary thing, having the practical purposes of giving and receiving general information, of meeting new people, and of taking one's part in decisions that have to be made. In populous places this will be a sizable group, probably a luncheon meeting with a speaker. The formal teaching value will depend largely on the quality of the speaker. Then there is the meeting of pastors of various churches in a town or city, usually once a month. This is an unpredictable thing, depending on the persons involved at any given time and on the nature of the leadership. The temptation for such a varied group is to settle for the least common denominator or to be moralistic. But it does provide a common meeting ground, probably the only one for that group of ministers when a matter of importance for the whole community arises. The leadership in such a meeting usually rotates and one can always use his turn to steer the program into what he considers real issues.

A more workable sort of group is a regular meeting of the pastors of the same church body in a natural geographical area. Such a meeting is small enough to have a meeting of minds, homogeneous enough to be free, varied enough in schools of thought to be lively. A group of this kind met at my house once a month, September to June, for almost ten years. Lunch was provided at cost and during it general concerns were discussed as they happened to come up. After lunch a paper was read by one of the members in rotation. There were two rules about the paper: it must concern itself with something of importance in the minister's life and work, and it must be a subject on which the writer had an opinion, for or against. The reader of the paper led the discussion, summarized it, and closed the meeting with prayers of his own choice. Frequently one paper grew out of another. In the course of ten years the membership of the group was constantly changing, bringing fresh insights to a nucleus of old-timers and balance to newcomers. Guests were always welcome. Those meetings were one of the most valuable and enjoyable experiences of my ministry.

Most men a few years out of seminary are tempted to become intellectually lazy and spiritually fat. The pastor is caught up in all sorts of busyness, some necessary, some thrust upon him, some invented by himself. In his seminary years he gathered a considerable body of knowledge, enjoyed contact with stimulating minds, probably discovered a field of special interest which he would like to develop. At moments he knew the genuine joy of study, the fire of curiosity, the detective interest in pursuing a truth to its roots. He may have thought of teaching as his life-work in the ministry. During this time he had to make up his mind, at least tentatively, about a number of things. If a man has read a small text in theology he can lecture safely in this field all his life, changing the illustrations from time to time. His difficulty comes when he reads two books. And by the time he has read three, or has listened to conflicting expositions, he has a growing awareness that either he must embrace a school of thought and pull it in after him or go through the costly and demanding process of deciding what he himself thinks about a number of basic questions. The Christian faith is not an easy faith to hold nor is it an inevitable tunnel from which there is only one coming-out place. It is a dare, a way of life, a trust.

All of this the man has sensed, some of it he has known. Then in his humanness he is tempted to forget about it, to settle for less, to keep the machinery moving and quietly go to seed. It is a form of suicide which is socially acceptable and sometimes welcomed by people who want to be comforted but not disturbed.

I used to counsel students to read when they were young, as I myself was counseled, to seize the gift of time in a small parish or mission for laying down a foundation of reading and study.

They tell me now that this is a fraud, that there is no such gift of time even in the smallest place. This may be true. It is certainly true that the better the pastor the greater will be the demands upon him. But busy pastors do manage to read and study. The key is the man's own sense of responsibility, his own desire to grow. After that the considerations are practical ones. I have no solution to this problem for myself or others but I shall venture a few suggestions.

Time for study must be made and, if possible, it should happen every day. The field of special interest is a good thing to foster; it is a growing edge. Wide reading is desirable as well as special reading. If one is a slow reader there are helpful courses in many universities to correct this. One should be working away most of the time at one of the great books in the faith. Mark Twain says that the classics are the books that everybody wants to have read and nobody reads. A little at a time will do it.

I have already spoken about reading with a notebook. There are other reading systems, some of them elaborate, which are worth trying. Bishop Craig Stewart worked out one for himself. He would mark a passage which caught his attention in a book he was reading, then write a key word and the page number on the back fly leaf. Later he made a card index by subjects, indicating on each card the book titles and page numbers where the references occurred. The first part of this system, even without the card index, makes useful passages more available. The real point is to keep on reading and thinking and questioning. Given that, a personal system for remembering ideas will probably provide itself.

There are good theological libraries in most parts of the country and most of them will lend books, or even mail them, to clergymen. Good summer courses are to be found in many places, frequently with first-rate teachers. There are stimulating journals of religious thought published here and in Europe.

The teaching ministry, which means the learning ministry, is one of the roots of usefulness in the Lord. About four hundred years ago Erasmus, the scholar of Rotterdam, wrote these words:

'Tis a brave world, my young masters and bachelors and doctors! Do not be afraid of it; do not calculate your chances so closely that you miss your chance; do not pretend to know what you do not know. Work and laugh and give thanks, for these three are one. You did not make the world. You cannot remake it. You cannot even spoil it. You may, indeed, have the felicity of improving some small corner of it, but in general the world has been pronounced "very good." Enter into its joy.[5]

FIVE ❁ THE PRIEST

When I was a seminarian a story went the rounds about a senior who had been ordained during his last semester. One day soon after his ordination he dressed himself with loving care in his new black suit, his spotless white collar, his well-polished shoes, and contemplated himself in the mirror. The effect was pleasing. Deciding to take the air in his glory he adjusted his new black hat and strolled into the world, that is to say, Ninth Avenue in New York City. As he stood on the curb, hands in pockets, wondering what to do next, he was observed by a drunk who seemed unimpressed. Their eyes met and the drunk from his near-horizontal position said, "Sonny, what the hell do you know about God?" The young man, to his credit, made no reply but went back to his room, took off his new clothes, and wondered what he did know about God.

To go back to our role images, the most satisfying and at the same time the most disturbing, is that of the apostle. The apostolic image is satisfying because it represents the heart of the ministry as we have received it—messenger, reconciler, missionary, father in God. It is disturbing because it makes more demands than a man can fulfill. The best intentions, the most thorough training, the most modern equipment will not fill the gap. Only God will. Whom God calls He sustains and empowers. A clergyman friend of mine working on New York's East Side once asked a boy on the street what he thought a priest was for. The boy said, "A priest is to pray."

Prayer is another way of saying dependence on God and that is what the Christian ministry exists to be and teach and do. Consider the alternatives. One may have a successful ministry because he is good or bright or strong or well-intentioned! The ordained man is the same person he was before ordination. In that act he dedicates all of his powers and possibilities to the service of God and the people of God, and he is blessed for a use. His needs are the same as before but perhaps more insistent since his is a representative ministry, both of and to his people. At the heart of all his needs is the need to be forgiven. Compared to the holiness of God all men are equally sinful. St. Augustine says that had there been but one sinner in the world Christ would have died for him. This the priest knows, as he knows that there is but one priesthood, that of our Lord, in which we partake.

It is almost always a surprise for people to learn as part of the Christian revelation that a man is important not because he is wise or strong or rich or famous, nor because of the opposite of any of these, but because God made him and redeemed him. Because he is a created soul for whom Christ died. Because he *is* and God *is* and *does*. A man is important because he is beloved of God. It is possible for a man to have a ministry, to partake in the eternal priesthood of Jesus Christ, because of the fact of the Cross—the same stumbling block, the same foolishness now as when St. Paul wrote to the Corinthians.

When one looks at our Lord's life of prayer as recorded in the gospel accounts one sees three things. The first is that he prayed in all the crises of His ministry. After His baptism, facing the realization of His Messiahship and the beginning of His public ministry, He went into a desert place to be alone with God. Something more was involved here than the wish to be quiet and think. Mark says (after the baptism), *"The Spirit immediately drove him out into the wilderness"* (1:12). Matthew

has, "*Then Jesus was led up by the Spirit into the wilderness . . .*" (4:1). Luke says, "*Jesus . . . was led by the Spirit
for forty days in the wilderness . . .*" (4:1). This prayer in
crisis is a dialogue; the first speaker is God, "the Spirit," to
whom Jesus in His manhood responds. In this meditation He
faces temptation—to be a magician providing bread for His
people, to be a spectacular superman claiming popular attention,
to "do a little evil that good may result"—and He resists it in
order to be the instrument of God's redeeming love as God may
choose to work it out. Again, as the demands of His public
ministry began to increase, He went away by Himself. "*And in
the morning, a great while before day, he rose and went out to a
lonely place, and there he prayed*" (Mk. 1:35). "*He went out
into the hills to pray; and all night he continued in prayer to
God*" (Lk. 6:12). Toward the close of His ministry, when the
end is in sight, we find Him again alone in Gethsemane, praying
that He may be able to do God's will. "*. . . remove this cup
from me; yet not what I will, but what thou wilt*" (Mk. 14:36).
In the loneliness of the Cross itself His prayer is to God, even in
anguish.

Secondly, time after time in the press of events, in the midst
of demands He "looked up to heaven," as if taking God by the
hand, and found power. His whole busy ministry, as reported by
the Evangelists, is marked by these "arrow" prayers.

Finally, His life of prayer and His life of other activity were
the same thing. He knew God's presence from moment to
moment, whatever was going on, and showed it forth sometimes
in words, sometimes in actions, sometimes in being. The inclu-
siveness of His concern and its relationship to the whole of life
is expressed in the prayer which He taught us.

There is a guide here for each of us in his ministry. In any
language the verb "to pray" means "to ask" or "beseech." It
does not necessarily have any religious connotation. It takes on
such a meaning when power is invoked, whether from a god or
a demon. A man can pray to the wrong god or for the wrong
things to his own destruction. The operating questions in the
use of prayer are "to whom?" and "for what?" In Jesus Christ

the Christian finds personally revealed the nature of the God of the Bible and a demonstration of the relationship of God and man at its best. Prayer is not the source of power; God is. Prayer to God is a way of saying that we know this is true and that we stand in need. For Christians it is an acknowledgment that they are living in God, and that they need His help to do His will. At the heart of it, prayer to God is thanksgiving.

The man of God, in his own crises, will pray to God as revealed in Christ because he has to. Sometimes this will be a lonely business and it may involve a temporary separation from his normal concerns. Young men facing ordination will want some time by themselves. Ordained men facing their own guiltiness, priests muffled by routine busyness, will need a time in the wilderness. The seventeenth-century divines knew about this. Witness: "Never less alone than when alone," and "Shutter the windows that the house may be full of light." This is a necessary thing, a blessing. Similarly, in the daily grist of the ministry we send arrow prayers to God our Father in our immediate needs: before making a sermon and before preaching it, on the way to make a call, before a conference, before a service of worship, in the face of opposition, and in time of trial. In all of these occasions, and with whatever words, we ask God to help us do our best for His sake and to His glory. Jeremy Taylor says, "I had rather your prayers be often than long." In time this attitude of dependence on God, this personal application of the words "through Jesus Christ our Lord," comes to color a man's whole life. His life of prayer and his life begin to become the same thing.

We really pray when we *have* to pray; anything up to that necessity is "saying prayers." We have to pray when we acknowledge our own inadequacy and at the same time God's readiness to empower us for His good purposes. We are reminded of these things when we pray with the Church. The great collects sink in. Phrases from the psalms and from the prayers of the daily offices become a part of our spiritual bloodstream. They speak to us in our condition of the goodness and the givenness of God. Because of this we can *"pray and not lose heart"* (Lk. 18:1).

Petition states a need as God's child, beginning with "our daily bread"; intercession follows the heart. The pastor will remember in God the persons for whom he is especially concerned—couples recently married, people in trouble who have honored him with their confidence, the difficult, the fractious, and those to whom he has ministered inadequately. He may have a list—he probably will have—but he will not talk about it. He will use it, and as intercession follows the heart so practical involvement follows intercession in a godly circle.

The problems of prayer are the same for any Christian before or after ordination. Here is a small bouquet of excerpts from the letters of four young men in their first cures. One writes, "Prayers? Can't remember when I *really* said them last. Did pretty well in seminary but now it's so easy to be busy. That's what's the trouble. We're too busy being busy. I think maybe there are two kinds of clergymen. The kind that say their prayers so that they don't have to do their work and the kind that try to do their work so that they don't have to say their prayers. That's not fair, though, is it? Because there must be people who get their work done because they say their prayers. It's always something I'm going to do."

Another man says, "I am beginning to see that a prayer and Bible-reading discipline every day is the most important thing in my life. Unless I do that I am as rattled as anybody else and am worth nothing to my people. Yet it is the easiest thing to let slip for often it does not accomplish immediate results."

A third man writing to friends at seminary says, "Get in the habit of saying your prayers. . . . Honestly it is the only strength that you have. God does speak to you if you keep quiet long enough to listen."

The fourth, a little older than the others, writing to a friend who is about to be ordained, says, "I was always told that prayer must be at the center of my life as a priest, and I could see that was true. I wanted it to be true for me, but I didn't see that it would be a changed truth as time went on. Being a priest is something quite different from what you thought it would be. I had made a mental picture of myself as a priest in the years before my ordination, and after ordination I tried to bring the picture alive. Then one day I knew the picture had faded out and that I had failed to make myself the priest I wanted to be. And 'the prayers of a priest,' as I had conceived them, had faded too. But the picture had had to be destroyed because it was the picture of a self-made priest and God in His mercy had destroyed it. It didn't seem very merciful at the time, for what was there left? There was one thing left: the knowledge that God doesn't use a self-made priest. For a priest is at the disposal of God. He may appear to be an acceptable official of an institution, but that is not the same thing. He may have multiplied his prayers into numerous acts of piety, but his acts of piety however edifying to others or to himself, do not necessarily put him at the disposal of God."

We are tempted to do various things but we are not tempted to say our prayers. Natural man believes in himself. It is only after a series of inner defeats that we come to trust in the Lord and mean it. Even then we will know spiritual dryness, wanderings of mind, the sense of the loss of God's presence, the night devils of futility and hypocrisy. When I was in seminary we had as a guest one semester an elderly English priest, a mature and gentle person whose rooms became a gathering place for students. One evening after a number of us had wandered in the conversation came around to what each of us would like to accomplish in his ministry. The visions were for the most part modest but all of them carried a hopeful flavor of recognition that the deed was worth doing. During the conversation each of us had anticipated what our guest would have to say. Finally, when it came his turn he said, "Sometime before I die I should like to say one good Our Father."

I think this about sums it up. God is good and patient and God is provoked every day. He will wait us out. He is "more ready to hear than we to pray." But our life is in Him and our usefulness. When we lead a retreat or a quiet day of meditation and prayer our people will catch from us whatever we have learned of His goodness. One does not flutter after holiness but the holiness of God is there to be found.

The man of God is subject to the same temptations that beset other men. After ordination the Seven Deadly Sins are still open to him, some of them perhaps more so than before. In the exercise of his ministry he will sometimes find himself in dangerous situations and while it is not sinful to be tempted it is foolish to imagine that one is safe. The best defenses are one's own intentions in God and plain common sense. And in time of accusation a man's record to date is of more use to him than a skillful argument.

Besides the general run of temptations, the priest is vulnerable in particular to some which have a theological coloring, chief among them presumption and despair. Both of these are practical atheism; presumption says, "I am God," despair says, "There is no God." Every person secretly wants to be God. This is part of the meaning of the garden of Eden story, the nature of original sin which says, "I am a special case." But when one makes believe that he is God he is likely to act like the devil. It is not difficult to act like a god, especially when the role is offered to one. Human naturewise it is hard to turn down. But it is corrosive. Dr. Faustus and Parson Jones are separated only by the footlights. Again, the only defenses are motive and sense. When the clergyman's continuing motive to serve God and God's people is his own thankfulness for the loving-kindness of God toward him, he is less likely to fall into the trap of presumption. Consider the difference between loving a person, and loving oneself in that person's presence. Sense includes the sanity of seeing oneself in scale. One of my clergy friends says that his sins get less original all the time! The late Samuel Hoffenstein says,

> *Wherever I go,*
> *I go too,*
> *And spoil everything.*[1]

Presumption is full, despair is empty. It is cold, unnerving,

and bitter. Even God has gone away. It is the midnight devil
that whispers in a man's voice, "Why did we ever leave Egypt?
Why didn't I go into the newspaper business? Why didn't I stay
in it? My sermons are hack work, my teaching perfunctory, my
devotions sterile. I have no thirst for soul-saving. I don't even
care." One has attempted too much in the wrong name. Lack of
hope eventually boils down to the absence of hope in oneself. It
is the twin brother of presumption. But it may be a necessary
starting place toward maturity. In *The Brothers Karamazov* one
of the characters says, "There is no faith worthy of the name
that is not born out of despair." There comes a moment, or
many moments, when one takes in the truth that this is not his
ministry. It is the Lord's. Christ the Lord has already conquered
sin and death; who am I to say the battle is not worth fighting?
The man of God is involved in a fight but it is a good fight. It
is the Lord's. Let him roll out of bed onto his knees and begin
again.

In Dewar and Hudson's *Manual of Pastoral Psychology* there
occurs this passage:

The life of the clergyman affords endless opportunities for
that deadliest form of hypocrisy, self-deception. Vanity posing as
dignity, priggishness as self-respect, self-pity as the result of over-
work, meanness or slovenliness as asceticism, moral cowardice as
worldliness, as being all things to all men, insincerity as humility.
Who among us can say that these have no place in his life?[2]

Who indeed? There are those whose feelers are always out to
catch the slightest breath of negative criticism. There are those
who wallow in the luxury of cheap melancholy. Benjamin Jowett
is reported to have said of one of his clerical contemporaries,
"What time he spares from the adornment of his person he
devotes to the neglect of his duties." Pride is a wall, self-pity is
suicide, hurt feelings are a waste of time. Almighty God, "who
for us men and for our salvation came down from heaven," cannot afford to be proud. He made Himself small to reach us and
in Christ has given us all things necessary to our salvation and
to our ministry.

Looking in the mirror I shall comment on one other clerical failing. This is gossip. I doubt that the clergy gossip more than other groups of people but there is no doubt that it is professionally unbecoming and sometimes dangerous. The person who knows the "real" facts behind every deposition, the "real" reason for this man's resignation, how that man "really" got elected bishop, together with the names of the palace guard—this person is not untypical of natural man but as an exhibit of a man in Christ he is poison. Erasmus says that charity is to deserve well of all persons. St. Paul puts charity above miracles but charity *is* a miracle. It is the ability to love because one is loved, to forgive because one knows himself to be forgiven.

What are the marks of the man of God? I would say steadiness, patience, and faith. When St. Paul says, *"Therefore, my beloved brethren, be steadfast, immovable, always abounding in the work of the Lord, knowing that in the Lord your labor is not in vain"* (I Cor. 15:58), he is, among other things, stating the Christian doctrine of Providence. God, who made the world, has a plan for it in which all things meet. God has a holy perfect good will toward us which is our freedom. God "whose divine providence ordereth all things both in heaven and earth," has a plan for us which is our usefulness. The priest who gives inner assent to this, who knows it emotionally as well as intellectually, this man is free to be useful, to abound in the work of the Lord. He has many plans but he knows that they are true only when they square with God's order. He is willing to have his plan set aside, his pet project shelved, and to try it a different way or not at all. There is a flexibility about him which is not weakness. He is free to change because he is sure of God.

He has time—time for himself, time for people, time for God. When people come to him, even when he had planned to do something else, they have his attention. He is there, he is listening, he is unhurried. He gets things done. He has time because he is not working against himself. He knows that he can be fooled and that he is sometimes a fool but in the midst of everything he knows that God is trustworthy. He can afford to be steady because he trusts God. The work of the ministry gets done not by geniuses or spectacular performers, but by ordinary people—like the apostles—who carry on consistently and cheerfully, with steadiness.

The man of God is able to wait. He does not take his pulse. He does not pull up his tender plants to see if they have roots yet. He wants things to happen, to grow, to mature, but he is willing to wait them out. After a while, he may even develop a little patience regarding himself without giving up the struggle and without settling down in the bog of complacency. There was a well-weathered clergyman who was persuaded by his bishop to leave the place where he had been for sixteen years and where he was pastor to the town, to take over a city parish which had memories of past splendor and was now surrounded by slums. Just before the depression this parish had built a monumental parish house with all sorts of modern equipment. The debt was enormous and unpaid. There were those who believed the parish should have moved out to greener pastures when the neighborhood changed. There were those who thought otherwise. Most of the people, stunned by their own losses, felt bewildered and not very hopeful about the church situation. On his first Sunday the newly arrived man preached a forthright sermon. Let the Church be the Church, he said, opening wide its doors and welcoming in the whole depressed community because they lived there. The next morning he received an indignant elder parishioner who had heard the sermon. She swept into his study and announced, "I think you are an old fool." Quite unmoved the priest replied, "There's no doubt about it. I've known it for years. What's your evidence?" Well, as it happened, she stayed and eventually became a Christian. The point of the story is, of course, that the man was speaking the precise truth. He *was* an old fool. God uses fools to get His work done; He doesn't have anybody else. A Christian is a redeemed fool.

I know of a diocese where the bishop—a wise and patient chief pastor—has made it a practice deliberately to take on from time to time men who have not been "successes" elsewhere. He sees them frequently, especially during the first year or two, supporting, counseling, guiding. Rarely has one of these men not found himself and his place in the ministry.

The man of patience does not always have an answer but he is willing to wait for one and is unsurprised when it turns out to be different from what he expected. He knows that there are many things which he cannot settle, that many situations resolve themselves by being left strictly alone, that a flare-up of temper when met with forbearance often translates itself into something very like gentleness. He knows that the only real defense is no defense at all. Persistent patience wins battles for the Lord when a head-on attack achieves nothing but estrangement.

One of the key words in the Christian ministry is the word "continue." Jesus says, *"Ye are they which have continued with me in my temptations"* (Lk. 22:28). St. Luke says of the disciples, *"And they continued stedfastly in the apostles' doctrine and fellowship, and in breaking of bread, and in prayers"* (Acts 2:42). St. James says, *"But whoso looketh into the perfect law of liberty, and continueth therein, he being not a forgetful hearer, but a doer of the work, this man shall be blessed in his deed"* (Jas. 1:25). The word is repeated in the services of the Church. In baptism the Church says, "We receive this child into the congregation of Christ's flock; and do sign him with the sign of the Cross, in token that hereafter he shall not be ashamed to confess the faith of Christ crucified, and manfully to fight under his banner, against sin, the world, and the devil; and to *continue* Christ's faithful soldier and servant unto his life's end." In confirmation the Church says, "Defend, O Lord, this thy child with thy heavenly grace; that he may *continue* thine for ever; and daily increase in thy Holy Spirit more and more, until he come unto thy everlasting kingdom." In the eucharistic thanksgiving are the familiar words, "And we humbly beseech thee, O heavenly Father, so to assist us with thy grace, that we may *continue* in that holy fellowship, and do all such good works as thou hast prepared for us to walk in."

The man of God is a man of faith. *"By faith Abraham, when he was called to go out into a place which he should after receive for an inheritance, obeyed; and he went out, not knowing whither he went"* (Heb. 11:8). *"By faith [Moses] forsook Egypt, not fearing the wrath of the king; for he endured, as seeing him who is invisible"* (Heb. 11:27). St. Paul writes to the Corinthians, *"For we walk by faith, not by sight"* (II Cor. 5:7). The basic Christian choice is the choice for God, against self. In one symbol or another natural man believes in himself; his strength, his luck, his intelligence, his ability not to be fooled. The Christian believes in God who is the source of his strength and his intelligence, the grounds of his being, his salvation when he acts like a fool. The choice is made many times. Self-respect is a by-product of God's respect for us. Belief in oneself and one's abilities and one's usefulness is a good thing when it is offered to God who is its source.

When I was a Fellow at The General Seminary I once sat in on an informal meeting of the faculty when a recent national church gathering was being discussed. Various people had given various opinions. Finally, the dean turned to Frank Gavin who had been silent up to that time and asked him for his opinion. "Well," he said, "when everything else fails you can always fall back on the Christian religion." The Christian religion ultimately rests on an act of faith. It is demonstrable but not provable. It is a personal act of faith in a Person.

Faith involves an act of trust in the work of Christ. In practice this means willingness to accept forgiveness. It is always more difficult to receive a gift than to give one, especially when the gift is offered at personal sacrifice. The gift of forgiveness offered us by God in Christ is the most costly gift there is. It can be received only in humbleness and thanksgiving. If one thinks of himself as the greatest sinner in the world that is not humbleness; it is pride. But when one begins to accept himself as a sinner for whom Christ died, to accept his acceptance in God, that is the beginning of his freedom. His faith begins to make him whole.

This is a battle. Judas could not accept the innocence of Jesus until he had betrayed Him and then, for him, it was too late. God is willing to be our last choice, after we have followed every other road, but in the end we have to do the choosing ourselves.

God in His mercy has already chosen us but He will not coerce us. If we knowingly choose against Him forever He will sustain us while we do so and we will be in hell. All of us choose wrongly at times, many have not yet *"resisted unto blood, striving against sin"* (Heb. 12:4), but when we do come into the blessedness of forgiveness it is through faith in the living God.

Sometimes our excursions into faith are tentative; like Nicodemus we come to Jesus by night posing hypothetical questions but stopping short of commitment. Sometimes they are superficial, like the little girl who knew God loved her because "she tried Him on a daisy." Sometimes they are casual as in the old phrase, "if you repent, more or less, of your sins, so to speak, you will be saved, after a fashion." Sometimes they are blasphemous. The dying Heinrich Heine when asked if he thought God would forgive him is said to have replied, "Of course He will forgive me. That's His business."

Faith is expectancy. "Be it unto thee according to thy *expectancy.*" Most of us expect so little. We distrust God because we make Him in the image of our own disillusionment. The promises of God exceed anything that we can ask or imagine and at the heart of all of them is the promise of Himself—the good companionship of God in Christ which makes all other good companionship possible and desirable.

The man of faith knows this and shows it forth. He has lots to give away but chiefly the knowledge of the goodness of God. Because of this people matter for him. He sees them, not in all of their unattractiveness, but as they may be—the clear picture within the blurred image. He improves situations by existing in them. His heart is in heaven but his feet are planted firmly on the ground. He is strong enough to be gentle. He is prepared for the world of "action and liability."

The recognition of complicity is the beginning of innocence,
The recognition of necessity is the beginning of freedom,
The recognition of the direction of fulfillment is death of self
And the death of self is the beginning of selfhood.[3]

One of the marks of our time is the development of the discipline which has come to be called pastoral psychology. Stirred by the theories of Freud, Jung, Adler, and others about the nature and uses of the unconscious, and armed with new methods of testing, we have been able to increase the effectiveness of all sorts of counselors. Vocational, industrial, and educational counselors as well as social workers have gained from new insights into the workings of the human mind. We still know very little about these things—a fact of which the wisest among psychologists and psychiatrists are careful to remind us—but we have come far enough to begin to have a general acceptance of basic ideas and terms. It is natural and commendable that a profession such as ours, closely related to human problems, should take advantage of new knowledge and new methods in dealing with them.

This movement had just begun to gather momentum when I was a student in seminary. When I enrolled in a course of clinical training in 1934, it was definitely a new thing and feeling its way. Hospital staffs were not sure what to do with us, but pioneers such as Richard Cabot and Anton Boisen helped to interpret needs and hopes. In those days there was a danger, born of enthusiasm, of amateur psychologizing; we loved the new words. This danger is still present but seems to be lessening. At present most seminaries offer courses making use of this new knowledge. Clinical training has become normative and in some places it is required. Books by the hundreds are available on various aspects of pastoral psychology and several professional journals in this field publish matters of current interest.

The pastoral counselor is an old figure in Hebrew and Christian literature. The word "counselor" is used in the contemporary sense more than twenty times in the Bible. Isaiah uses it as a part of the description of the wise ruler who was to come. *"His name shall be called . . . Counsellor"* (Isa. 9:6). There are many instances of people coming to Jesus for counsel and interpretation. All through Christian history the figure of the pastoral counselor, the spiritual director, is a familiar one. The practice of the sacrament of penance has always involved counseling. Indeed, pastoral psychology has been called the Protestant confessional. Counseling has always been a part of the Christian ministry and always will be. The science of pastoral theology, the cure of souls, is an old one which has its own history, disciplines and resources. Pastoral psychology is a new science which is only just beginning to develop self-consciousness and direction. It has some good things to teach us—in the way of motivation for behavior, for instance. There is also a large and useful older literature on the subject in which young men would do well to read.

The man of God as counselor is both an old role and a new one. The term "psychosomatic," for instance, is fairly recent but the truth which it describes was used by the Church in the first century to combat the heresy of Gnosticism. It has always been true that perplexed people will seek out a godly man rather than a clever one. The man who has been quiet enough to learn a little of the ways of God will have some wisdom to offer. There are no new sins. This is why I am saying whatever I have to say about counseling under the heading of Priest. The best counselor will be the person who knows God best.

On the other hand, all truth is of God, whenever it makes its appearance. The new science of pastoral psychology has good and useful things to teach us. We begin to learn a little more about the motives of human behavior, about the layers of consciousness, about the nature of guilt and anxiety, about the meaning of physical and mental sickness. We have discovered that, among other things, clinical training is a help to self-knowledge and a timesaver. The end is the same pastoral end: freedom to choose, ability to relate to other people creatively, oneness with God. I have found it helpful and interesting to have a psychiatrist friend or two with whom I can discuss matters of mutual concern. Many psychiatrists have become Christians through such relationships. In some communities there are groups of psychiatrists and clergymen who meet together regularly. This is a growing movement and one from which both sides may learn.

It seems to me that the principles governing the man of God

as counselor are few and simple. I shall name them as I understand them. The wise counselor will be available. This may mean
actual places and clock time but it also means that this man
can be reached. He is accessible. He knows how to listen and he
listens more than he talks. He hears people out. Whenever possible he avoids being judgmental, knowing that to be God's
province. If there comes a time when he must judge, he does so
as honestly as he can and he does not enjoy it. He knows that
people have a right to be the way they are and that his acceptance of them as they are (as God accepts each of us) may be
the very gift of freedom which makes it possible for them to
change. He does not manipulate people or try to make them over
in his own image.

People have a right to privacy. There is a lot of difference
between a closed door and a locked door. This will be governed
by the canon of common sense. The church itself is a good
place in which to listen to people; private because it is public.
Interviews may often end with prayers, however informal, com-
mending this person and his problem to God's wisdom and
compassion.

The wise counselor does not play God. To the best of his
ability and as a redeemed sinner he represents God in Christ
who *"is come to seek and to save that which was lost"* (Lk.
19:10). A young man in the ministry is pleased when people
come to seek his counsel. It helps him to feel that he is being
useful, even to dramatize himself to himself as a wise counselor.
After a while one develops a vast incuriosity about his people.
He neither hopes that they will come to him nor that they will
not. This means, of course, that they are free to come if and
when they need to. He keeps their confidences. He is trustworthy.

In all things, at all times, and in all places, the man of God is
God's representative in the world. As pastor or administrator, as
preacher or teacher, as priest standing at the altar to offer the
sacrifice of praise and thanksgiving, declaring the forgiveness of
God, blessing the people in God's name, he is the same man. He
is a man in Christ. *"Therefore seeing we have this ministry, as
we have received mercy, we faint not"* (II Cor. 4:1).

NOTES

Chapter Two. *The Administrator*

[1] V. A. Demant, *Theology of Society* (London: Faber, 1947), p. 11.
[2] George Michonneau, *Revolution in a City Parish* (West-minister, Md.: Newman, 1952), pp. 20–21.
[3] Pamphlet: *The Vestry and Commission Plan* (Trinity Church, Concord, Mass., 1954), p. 1.
[4] Walter J. Carey, *My Priesthood* (London: Longmans, 1918), p. 36.

Chapter Three. *The Preacher*

[1] Theodore O. Wedel, *The Pulpit Rediscovers Theology* (Greenwich, Conn.: Seabury, 1956), p. 4.
[2] George Santayana, *Character and Opinion in the United States* (New York: Scribner, 1922), p. vii.
[3] T. S. Eliot, *The Rock* (New York: Harcourt, Brace, 1934), p. 9.
[4] Artie Shaw, *The Trouble with Cinderella* (New York: Farrar, Straus and Young, 1952), p. 143.
[5] Margaret Widdemer, *Hill Garden* (New York: Rinehart, 1936), copyright 1936 by Margaret Widdemer. Reprinted by permission of the publisher.

[6] St. Augustine, *De catechizandis rudibus* (Chap. 2, translated by Clement Rogers).

[7] Erich Fromm, *The Forgotten Language* (New York: Rinehart, 1951), p. 3.

Chapter Four. *The Teacher*

[1] Dorothy L. Sayers, *Creed or Chaos* (London: Methuen, 1947), copyright 1947 by Dorothy L. Sayers, pp. 21–23. Reprinted by permission of the publisher.

[2] George Santayana, *Character and Opinion in the United States* (New York: Scribner, 1922), p. 47.

[3] James Thurber, *Further Fables for Our Time* (New York: Simon and Schuster, 1956), p. 169.

[4] William Temple, *The Church Looks Forward* (New York: Macmillan, 1934), p. 30.

[5] Desiderius Erasmus, *De pueris instituendis* (1529, translator unknown).

Chapter Five. *The Priest*

[1] Samuel Hoffenstein, *Pencil in the Air* (Garden City, New York: Doubleday, 1947), p. 15.

[2] Lindsay Dewar and Cyril E. Hudson, *A Manual of Pastoral Psychology* (London: Philip Allan, 1932), p. 98.

[3] Robert Penn Warren, *Brother to Dragons* (New York: Random House, 1953), p. 214. Reprinted by permission of the publisher.

Set in Linotype Electra
Format by Nancy Etheredge
Manufactured by The Haddon Craftsmen, Inc.
Published by HARPER & BROTHERS, *New York*